Toward Freedom

The Jacobin series features short interrogations of politics, economics, and culture from a socialist perspective, as an avenue to radical political practice. The books offer critical analysis and engagement with the history and ideas of the Left in an accessible format.

The series is a collaboration between Verso Books and *Jacobin* magazine, which is published quarterly in print and online at jacobinmag.com.

Toward Freedom

The Case against Race Reductionism

TOURÉ F. REED

VERSO
London • New York

First published by Verso 2020
Touré F. Reed © Verso 2020

3 5 7 9 10 8 6 4 2

Verso
UK: 6 Meard Street, London W1F 0EG
US: 20 Jay Street, Suite 1010, Brooklyn, NY 11201
versobooks.com

Verso is the imprint of New Left Books

ISBN-13: 978-1-78663-438-2
ISBN-13: 978-1-78663-440-5 (US EBK)
ISBN-13: 978-1-78663-439-9 (UK EBK)

British Library Cataloguing in Publication Data
A catalogue record for this book is available from the British Library

Library of Congress Cataloging-in-Publication Data
A catalog record for this book is available from the Library of Congress

Typeset in Fournier MT by Hewer Text UK Ltd, Edinburgh
Printed in the UK by CPI Group (UK) Ltd, Croydon CR0 4YY

To my grandparents, Clarita M. Reed and
Adolph L. Reed Sr., and my father, Adolph L. Reed Jr.

CONTENTS

LIST OF ABBREVIATIONS

ACA	Affordable Care Act
AFB	American Farm Bureau
AFDC	Aid to Families with Dependent Children
AFL	American Federation of Labor
ARA	Area Redevelopment Act
ARRA	American Recovery and Reinvestment Act
BLM	Black Lives Matter
BPP	Black Panther Party
BSCP	Brotherhood of Sleeping Car Porters
CAP	Community Action Program
CCC	Civilian Conservation Corps
CEA	Council of Economic Advisers
CETA	Comprehensive Employment and Training Act
CIO	Congress of Industrial Organizations
CORE	Congress of Racial Equality
CP	Communist Party
ED	Department of Education
DOL	Department of Labor
EAC	Emergency Advisory Councils

EEOC	Equal Employment Opportunity Commission
EFCA	Employee Free Choice Act
EITC	Earned Income Tax Credit
EPA	Environmental Protection Agency
FEPC	Fair Employment Practices Committee
FHA	Federal Housing Administration
FLSA	Fair Labor Standards Act
FRG	Federal Republic of Germany
HUAC	House Un-American Activities Committee
HUD	Housing and Urban Development (Department)
JCNR	Joint Committee on National Recovery
LDF	Legal Defense Fund of the NAACP
MDTA	Manpower and Development Training Act
MOWM	March on Washington Movement
NAACP	National Association for the Advancement of Colored People
NAFTA	North American Free Trade Agreement
NALC	Negro American Labor Council
NIRA	National Industrial Recovery Act
NLRA	National Labor Relations Act
NLRB	National Labor Relations Board
NNA	New Negro Alliance
NNC	National Negro Congress
NRA	National Recovery Administration
NUL	National Urban League
PWA	Public Works Administration
PWOC	Packinghouse Workers' Organizing Committee
SCAD	State Commission Against Discrimination (New York)

SCLC	Southern Christian Leadership Conference
SNCC	Student Nonviolence Coordinating Committee
SSA	Social Security Act
SWOC	Steel Workers' Organizing Committee
TARP	Troubled Asset Relief Program
TPP	Trans-Pacific Partnership
TSLU	Tobacco Stemmers and Laborers' Union
UAW	United Auto Workers
VA	Veterans Administration
VISTA	Volunteers in Service to America
WB	Workers' Bureau
WC	Workers' Councils
WPA	Works Progress Administration/Work Projects Administration

INTRODUCTION: THE ERA OF RACE REDUCTIONISM

The 2016 campaign for the Democratic presidential nomination condensed around two distinct visions of social justice. One, advanced by Hillary Clinton and the party's corporate wing, accepted the limits of the neoliberal regime of upward redistribution even as it embraced fairness for nonwhites, women, gender-nonconforming people and other specified populations within the system. The other, asserted by Bernie Sanders, reaffirmed the public-good framework—established during the New Deal and carried through the postwar period—that was crucial to both the exponential growth of the American middle class and the modern civil rights movement.

Although I enthusiastically cast my ballot for Sanders in Illinois's 2016 Democratic primary and look forward to voting for him again in 2020, when Senator Bernie Sanders announced his presidential campaign in April 2015, I feared the Democratic Party and the corporate media would succeed in their efforts to cast him as a novelty candidate. I have always appreciated Sanders's politics, but I had presumed that a quarter-century of neoliberal hegemony had crowded out space for a return to the public-good-oriented domestic agenda that he championed.

To be clear, I refer to Sanders's platform as "public-good-oriented" rather than "democratic socialist," not because I have an aversion to socialism or dispute the candidate's self-identity and long political history on the left. Rather, casting Sanders as a democratic socialist or social democrat obscures the fact that the Bernie Sanders who campaigned for the Democratic nomination ran on a platform in step with the best of New Deal liberalism.

Today, Sanders's calls for free public higher education, universal health care, tax hikes on the nation's wealthiest individuals and corporations, massive reinvestment in the nation's infrastructure and an invigorated union movement sound like a plan to infuse alien Scandinavian social democratic policies into American democracy. However, in the 1930s and 1940s and even in the quarter-century or so following World War II—the era that most Americans reflexively think of as the golden age of the middle class—Sanders's political platform would not have been so unusual for a Democratic presidential candidate.

During the New Deal (1933–40), American workers won a number of concessions from capital that would help pave the way for the postwar expansion of the nation's middle class. The National Labor Relations Act (NLRA), the Social Security Act (SSA) and the Fair Labor Standards Act (FLSA) would afford the workers covered by these laws: a much-strengthened right to collective bargaining; insulation from financial hardship wrought by termination, workplace injury, the loss of a wage earner, or just growing old; a forty-hour work week; and a floor below which workers' wages could not fall. In the same decade, the Federal Housing Administration (FHA) would create long-term mortgages, making homeownership possible for most white workers for the first time in the industrial era.

World War II dampened the New Deal's social democratic potential—which was always restrained by Roosevelt's overarching mission to create a sustainable model of capitalism—both by stifling labor and civil rights militancy and by displacing the "regulatory state" model of government stewardship of the nation's economy in favor of the more conservative, growth-oriented "compensatory state" model.[1] So, while the New Deal may have been as close to social democracy as the United States has ever been, the comparative strength of American capital by World War II ensured that New Deal liberalism would be far removed from socialism. Still, President Roosevelt and the New Dealers did advance a vision for a social corporatist democracy that sought to mitigate capitalism's harshest implications for American citizens while alleviating the tensions between industrial capitalism and republican democracy. Thus, in his final State of the Union on January 11, 1944, President Roosevelt laid out what he termed a "Second Bill of Rights," updated for the industrial age, which would establish the right to a job, a living wage, a decent home and health care.[2]

While Roosevelt's Second Bill of Rights was in step with the sensibilities of most Americans by the end of World War II, it would not come to pass. Indeed, by 1947, a combined

Republican and Dixiecrat congressional supermajority swiftly rolled back workers' rights and tamped down labor militancy. The Taft-Hartley Act (1947)—which eliminated the closed shop, card check and sympathy strikes while placing restrictions on unions', but not corporations', political activities—was crucial to this project.[3] But despite intense opposition from Republicans and conservative Southern Democrats, President Truman's 1948 presidential platform promised to build on the New Deal's economic liberalism. Truman's "Fair Deal" called for the repeal of Taft-Hartley, national health care, full-employment policies, the expansion of public works and comprehensive housing legislation. Truman would likewise become the first Democratic president to adopt a formal civil rights platform—which included a permanent Fair Employment Practices Commission and federal anti-lynching and voting rights legislation.[4]

Truman won reelection, but the combined Republican and Dixiecrat majority in Congress foreclosed the Fair Deal. Nevertheless, even Republican president Dwight Eisenhower's America continued to reflect the New Deal's influence. Indeed, by the late 1950s one-third of the workforce was unionized. Unionized workers, and even a growing number of nonunionized workers, had access to employer-sponsored health insurance plans—which major employers had just begun to establish as an alternative to a taxpayer-funded health care system. Robust state contributions to public higher education ensured that tuition at public universities was either free or extremely inexpensive. And the highest marginal income tax rate was about 91 percent.

In the mid-1960s, when the American middle class was on even firmer footing, the union movement was still strong; tuition at public universities remained either free or inexpensive, and the highest marginal income tax rate was then about 75 percent. The Johnson administration's Great Society, moreover, extended health care to two classes of Americans—the aged and the poor—who did not have the benefit of employer-sponsored health insurance.[5] And the public-good framework that informed the above would prove indispensable to the civil rights movement's major legislative victories—the Civil Rights Act of 1964, the Economic Opportunity Act (1964), the Voting Rights Act of 1965 and the Civil Rights Act of 1968—even if these acts were incapable of redressing the structural economic sources of racial disparities.

The Keynesian consensus—as the aforementioned period is called—birthed and nurtured the American middle class of lore. But the zeitgeist of that era was, in many ways, far removed from the political-economic orthodoxies of the conservative neoliberal era, ushered in by Margaret Thatcher and Ronald Reagan in the wake of stagflation (1973–75). Perceiving government intervention in labor and housing markets for the public good as an encumbrance on otherwise rational markets, neoliberal Republican *and* Democratic administrations—from Reagan to Trump and from Clinton to Obama—have, to one degree or another, whittled away at the social safety net, consumer protections and workers' rights that were the product of the Keynesian consensus.

The poor have certainly paid the price for neoliberalism's rejection of the public-interest model of governance, but so too have America's working and middle classes. Since the mid-1950s, the share of the American workforce that is unionized has declined from a high of more than 30 percent to fewer than 10 percent today.[6] The decline of the union movement has contributed to a massive upward redistribution of wealth since the late 1970s. In 1965, the average CEO earned forty times as much as the average worker; today, that number is more than 300 times as much. Since 1980, wages for the top 1 percent of wage earners have risen ten times faster than those of the bottom 90 percent of workers. Today, the top 5 percent of households possess nearly 75 percent of the nation's wealth, while the bottom 60 percent of American households have actually lost wealth over the past few decades. And the atrophy of the public sector—wrought by privatization schemes and tax breaks for the nation's wealthiest citizens and corporations—has not only contributed to the decay of America's infrastructure, but state budget cuts to public higher education have likewise resulted in soaring college tuition costs.[7]

All of this is to say that there really was an outsider candidate in 2016 who ran on a platform aimed at addressing the problems impacting working people in the United States, and his name was Bernie Sanders.

The pain inflicted on the nation's working and middle classes notwithstanding, I had presumed that a quarter-century of bipartisan commitment to neoliberalism's central doctrines ensured that a presidential campaign that sought to reinfuse New Deal liberalism into US politics would be crushed by corporate media and Democratic elites before it even got off the ground. So when Sanders announced his 2016 presidential campaign, I could never have imagined he would ultimately win twenty-three of fifty-seven Democratic primary contests. Even if the Democratic National Committee's (DNC's) decision to stack the deck of primary races in favor of Hillary Clinton was cause for outrage, the fact that Sanders's platform resonated with 43 percent of Democratic primary voters was cause for optimism about the prospects for a progressive political agenda capable of pushing back against the neoliberal assault on working people.

But if the strength of Sanders's primary challenge gave reason to believe that neoliberalism's grip on the electorate's political imagination had weakened, the Democratic and identitarian-left backlash to Sanders and his supporters revealed a deeply rooted reactionary tendency in contemporary liberal discourse related to race and inequality. Democrats and many self-identified progressives not only dismissed the utility of Sanders's platform for African Americans—characterizing his redistributive agenda as "class reductionist"—but they coalesced around putatively left identitarian formulations to attack his program from the right.

The charge that Sanders was a class reductionist was, and still is, a red herring. Desperate to shore up its support among black voters, the Clinton campaign deftly used identitarian constructs to deflect attention from the full implications of their commitment to market-friendly neoliberal policies. Representative James Clyburn (SC), for example, opposed Sanders's call for a return to taxpayer-funded (free) higher education by arguing that Sanders's plan—which Clyburn grossly mischaracterized—would hurt historically black colleges and universities (HBCUs) by diverting resources to publicly funded, predominantly white institutions (PWIs).[8] Clyburn, who sat on the board of a private HBCU, ignored the benefits of Sanders's proposal for both publicly funded HBCUs and the large number of poor and working-class African American students who can only finance their college education by taking on student loans.

Hillary Clinton likewise deployed the language of structural racism and intersectionality to obscure the impact of her husband's legislative agenda on disproportionately black voters. Without so much as a hint of irony, Secretary Clinton asserted that Sanders's calls for banking regulations and redistributive policies were of little importance to black and brown Americans as such proposals would do nothing to end the systemic racism that, she claimed, was the root cause of the subprime mortgage crisis and mass incarceration.[9] Beyond the fact that African Americans have been overrepresented among victims of predatory mortgage lending and the carceral state thanks, in no small part, to laws enacted by President Bill Clinton, regulation of the banking industry and the establishment of a living wage would likely do much to redress disparities in both wealth and the criminal justice system. Indeed, banking regulation could eliminate predatory lending altogether. And as political scientist Marie Gottschalk has shown, income inequality, cuts to state indigent legal services programs and the return of for-profit prisons are at the heart of African Americans' overrepresentation in the criminal justice system.

Curiously, liberal critics frequently cast Sanders's platform as anachronistic, but without any formal acknowledgment that he was simply calling for a return to the kind of public-interest approach to governance—ushered in by the Democratic party of Roosevelt—that not only grew the American middle class but had also helped lay the foundation for the civil rights movement. Those progressive critics who did reference American history, such as the acclaimed public intellectual Ta-Nehisi Coates, often did so to no good effect. Though Coates ultimately declared his support for Sanders, he too cast the Vermont senator as "class reductionist." Specifically, Coates rebuked Sanders for proposing a platform that sought to "ameliorate the effects of racism through broad, mostly class-based policies—doubling the minimum wage, offering single-payer health-care, delivering free higher education." According to Coates, Sanders's proposed redistributive policies were just "the same 'A rising tide lifts all boats' thinking that dominated Democratic anti-racist policy for a generation." Sanders's proposals thus, Coates claimed, suffered from the same wrongheaded presumption that doomed the War on Poverty—postwar liberals' refusal to acknowledge that racism was not merely "a relative of white poverty and inequality," but it was "an active, distinct evil" of its own.[10]

Coates's historical analogy failed on its merits, insofar as he conflated the Johnson administration's efforts to mitigate poverty via a conservative growth agenda with Sanders's progressive redistributive proposals. Still, had Sanders's platform been wed to calls to repeal extant antidiscrimination legislation, Coates's fear that blacks would not benefit equally from the Vermont senator's proposals might not have been unreasonable. However, Sanders did not run on a pledge to end or even "mend" affirmative action or any other antidiscrimination policies. The Democratic presidential candidate who had run on *that* platform was Secretary Clinton's husband.[11]

To be clear, I have no interest in relitigating the 2016 Democratic primary race. In fact, the specter of a Trump presidency not only motivated me to vote for Hillary Clinton in the general election, but I encouraged others to do the same.[12] Still, the 2016 Democratic primaries revealed a critical fault line within Democratic and progressive politics. Just as the popularity of Sanders's call for a return to a public-good-oriented approach to governance drew attention to a broad cross section of the electorate's disillusionment with a quarter-century of neoliberal hegemony, liberals' dismissal of Sanders as a "class reductionist" announced corporate Democrats' and a stratum of identitarian progressives' commitment to a class politics—shrouded in a language of identity and attitudes, uncoupled from political economy—that has long failed disproportionately black and brown working people.

There is little doubt that Secretary Clinton (much like Joe Biden, Kamala Harris and other contenders this time around) and her surrogates' strategic use of racial identity politics reflected the convergence of issues that were unique to the second decade of the twenty-first century. Sanders's strong showing in the Democratic primaries and caucuses forced the centrist-Clinton campaign to the rhetorical left on trade, education and wage policies. To counter the insurgency, Clinton needed to shore up her support with black voters, who were a reliable, economically diverse constituency that—as Clinton had learned in 2008—wielded disproportionate influence over Southern primaries. Clinton thus shrewdly wrapped herself in the legacy of the nation's first (neoliberal) black president—a strategy that would have been all the more appealing given Donald Trump's racist and xenophobic campaign stump—helping her win "the black vote" handily, despite the disproportionate damage inflicted upon African Americans by President Bill Clinton's welfare, criminal justice, labor and trade policies.[13]

Nevertheless, the specific issues informing the Clinton campaign's use of identity politics in the 2016 Democratic presidential primary were merely vulgar expressions of a long-standing and deeply problematic tendency in liberal thought and policy pertaining to race and inequality. Indeed, as I will explore in the chapters that follow, those who had claimed that Sanders was following in the long tradition of liberal "class reductionists" who have ignored systemic racism's impact on disparities were both mischaracterizing postwar antipoverty efforts and misidentifying the root causes of liberal policymakers' inability to redress racial inequities. Democratic presidential administrations—from Kennedy to Obama—have unquestionably failed to address the structural sources of racial disparities. However, far from reducing race to class, liberal social policy since the Cold War has tended to abstract racial disparities from the political-economic forces that generate them. Simply put, the deficiencies of postwar racial liberalism derive from its attachment to *race* reductionism, rather than class reductionism.

To be sure, liberals and progressives did not always separate race from class. Influenced by New Deal industrial democracy, civil rights and labor leaders of the 1930s and 1940s generally presumed that racism was inextricably linked to class exploitation. Civil rights leaders of this era thus identified interracial working-class solidarity as essential to racial equality.

The rightward turn in American politics ushered in by the Cold War would displace analyses of race rooted in political economy. By the 1950s, liberal thinkers and Democratic policymakers began to coalesce around culturalist conceptions of inequality that formally rejected race as a biological category but ultimately imputed a rigidity to ethnic group culture—uncoupling it from proximate material influences—that treated race as a social construct in name only. Drawing on concepts like ethnic pluralism/diversity and the culture of poverty/underclass ideology, late-Keynesian and neoliberal Democrats alike would trace racial disparities to whites' ingrained prejudices and poor blacks' cultural deficiencies.

Liberals' tendency to divorce race from class has had dire consequences for African American and other low-skilled workers. Specifically, race reductionism has obscured the political-economic roots of racial disparities, resulting in policy prescriptions that could have only limited value to poor and working-class blacks. Despite the fact that African Americans have long been overrepresented among unskilled workers and public-sector employees, postwar liberal policymakers have generally ignored the impact of issues such as automation, deindustrialization, public-sector retrenchment and the decline of the union movement on blacks. Instead, modern liberal antipoverty efforts have generally bound macroeconomic growth agendas to a mix of antidiscrimination policies, cultural tutelage, job training and punitive measures ranging from welfare reform to the carceral state. Thus, Democratic policymakers—from the War on Poverty through the postracial presidency of the nation's first black commander-in-chief— have not simply eschewed progressive redistributive economic policies in favor of conservative growth politics, they have in fact used a language of racial reductionism to advance this agenda.

The chapters that follow explore the trajectory of the liberal thought and policy related to inequality, outlined above, through examining race reductionist thinkers and policymakers —among them Oscar Handlin, Daniel Patrick Moynihan, Barack Obama[14] and Ta-Nehisi Coates—contrasted with economic structuralists—such as A. Philip Randolph, Bayard Rustin, Michael Harrington and Charles Killingsworth. Chapter 1 examines the class orientation of black politics during the New Deal and World War II. Chapter 2 explores the influence of ethnic pluralism over postwar racial liberalism via a critical analysis of the work of acclaimed immigration historian Oscar Handlin. Chapter 3 proffers a critique of the Moynihan Report that explicates the relationship between the Johnson administration's embrace of culturalist conceptions of inequality and the War on Poverty's rejection of the kind of redistributive policies advocated by contemporary labor-liberals and leftists such as Randolph, Rustin, Killingsworth and Harrington. Chapter 4 explores the complementary roles played by President Obama's postracial presidency and Ta-Nehisi Coates's reparations politics in bolstering support for neoliberalism's ongoing assault on public-good-oriented governance. And, finally, I conclude with some reflections on liberals' and left-identitarians' tightening embrace of race reductionist frameworks during the Trump presidency.

The unfolding 2020 Democratic primary makes clear that progressives will either reject race reductionism or reject the policies that can actually end racial disparities and other forms of inequality. There is, of course, no doubt that race/racism continues to adversely influence the lives of blacks and other people of color in the United States, ensuring the continued utility of antidiscrimination measures for the imaginable future. Still, given that the wages and wealth of the bottom 60 percent of American workers have been on a forty-year downward slide, a policy agenda that seeks only to redress disparities will be incapable of ending precarity for the masses of black and brown workers. If we hope to improve the material lives of poor and working-class black and brown people, we must demand a return to a public-good model of governance that presumes the general welfare necessitates not just antidiscrimination policies but a robust public sector and direct state intervention in labor and housing markets for the benefit of *all* of the nation's working people.

WHEN BLACK PROGRESSIVES DIDN'T SEPARATE RACE FROM CLASS

In the 1980s, president Ronald Reagan launched a racialized assault on the American welfare state. A Goldwater Republican, Reagan was philosophically opposed to the public interest model of government that had informed the New Deal and postwar liberalism. Though Reagan's hostility to entitlements helped deny him the Republican presidential nomination in 1976, four years later he understood that the breadth of support for entitlements—welfare programs whose eligibility requirements transcend class—precluded a direct assault on programs like Social Security's old age retirement benefits and Medicare. Instead, Reagan set his sights on hobbling means-tested programs—welfare programs whose beneficiaries are poor and disproportionately black and brown.

Reagan repealed President Nixon's Comprehensive Employment and Training Act (CETA) and cut funding to programs such as Aid to Families with Dependent Children (AFDC), Medicaid and Social Security Disability Insurance.[1] Reagan, who had been an outspoken critic of antidiscrimination legislation since the 1960s, also tried a number of schemes intended to undermine affirmative action. Despite his best efforts, Reagan failed to either narrow the scope of affirmative action compliance guidelines for government contractors or to end Nixon-era "goals and timetables." He was, however, able to curtail enforcement of antidiscrimination policy by both cutting funding to the Equal Employment Opportunity Commission (EEOC) and appointing Clarence Thomas, a well-known black critic of affirmative action, as its director.[2]

Reagan's assault on the American welfare state extended well beyond means-tested programs and antidiscrimination policies, as the nation's first neoliberal president slashed both income tax and corporate tax, deregulated the banking, energy, telecommunication and transportation industries, and undercut consumer protections as well as labor and environmental laws by either underfunding the relevant federal agencies or by cynically appointing antagonists to direct them. Still, there is no denying that Reagan used a language steeped in racial resentment to attack the welfare state through its soft underbelly, means-tested programs and antidiscrimination policy.

Indeed, Reagan and his followers' contention that permissive liberal social policies of the 1960s had spawned legions of parasitic black "welfare queens" who were bankrupting the nation one out-of-wedlock birth and tricked-out Cadillac at a time bound racial animus to economic anxiety in a narrative intended to nurture antistatist sensibilities among working-class and middle-class white Americans, whose prosperity was itself the product of the American welfare state.

As Reaganism became bipartisan consensus in the 1990s, scholars such as Michael K. Brown, Michael B. Katz, Jill Quadagno and Adolph L. Reed Jr. responded to neoliberalism's racialized attacks on welfare by drawing attention to the uneven distribution of the American welfare state's rewards. Specifically, they not only challenged the culturalist interpretations of poverty that informed the "welfare queen" and "crack baby" tropes, they also demonstrated the welfare state's crucial role—in the form of New Deal labor and housing policy, entitlements and state stewardship of postwar economic growth—in the creation of the *white* American middle class. Indeed, Brown, Katz, Quadagno and Reed made clear that the white middle class reaped the lion's share of the American welfare state's benefits via the NLRA, the FHA's mortgage policies, the GI Bill, the Federal-Aid Highway Act, entitlements and an elaborate private welfare system—including pensions and employer-sponsored health insurance—which most blacks had been denied access to thanks to discriminatory housing policies and employer and union discrimination (particularly in the elite building trades).[3]

Brown's, Katz's, Quadagno's and Reed's respective defenses of affirmative action and means-tested programs did not stop with the observation that state intervention in capitalist labor and housing markets had been crucially important to the expansion of the postwar white American middle class. To be sure, these left scholars were highly critical of New Democratic social scientists like Theda Skocpol, William Julius Wilson and Paul Starr, whose calls for universalism complemented the neoliberal assault on affirmative action and means-tested programs.[4] Nevertheless, Brown, Katz, Quadagno and Reed were clear that—given the disproportionate impact of dein-dustrialization, the decline of the union movement and public sector retrenchment on blacks—truly universal *redistributive* programs, implemented equitably with the aid of the Voting Rights Act and antidiscrimination policy, were the only effective means of ending economic and racial inequality. In other words, their historically grounded defenses of the types of programs that benefited blacks disproportionately were wed to a broader case for a return to the public-interest model of government that had fueled the postwar expansion of America's disproportionately white middle class.

As neoliberalism's grip on the liberal-left imagination tight-ened during the first two decades of the twenty-first century, however, a new generation of students of race and inequality took the bifurcation of the New Deal and postwar welfare states as evidence of the inherent limitations of universal programs. Historians Jefferson Cowie and Nick Salvatore, for example, posit what political scientist Cedric Johnson has termed the "constraint of race" thesis. Arguing that New Deal liberalism was restrained by racist Southern Democrats, Cowie and Salvatore ultimately contend that racism has perpetually hobbled broad, class-based redistributive reforms.[5]

Public intellectual Ta-Nehisi Coates has made much the same case. Drawing from the work of political scientist Ira Katznelson, Coates takes FHA mortgage discrimination and the SSA's exemptions for agricultural workers and domestic and personal servants as partial bases for his case for racial reparations—a redistributive agenda from which *only* African

Americans might benefit. Specifically, Coates contends that, since the late colonial period, working-class whites' pathological commitment to white-skin privilege has not only precluded interracial political alliances based on mutual economic interest, but ontological race/racism ensures that universal redistributive programs are incapable of redressing racial disparities.[6]

As I will discuss in detail in Chapter 4, the constraint of race thesis downplays capitalists' sway over New Deal labor and housing policies. What is no less problematic, however, is that the framework looks past the New Deal's much-studied, transformative effect on African American life and politics.

To be sure, New Deal programs, which were generally administered at the local level, were marred by discrimination. Nevertheless, millions of African Americans benefited from New Deal initiatives—sometimes in greater proportion than their share of the general population, even if they were underrepresented in relation to their need. Blacks were just 10 percent of the total population, for example, but accounted for 20 percent of all individuals on welfare rolls. Several hundred thousand African Americans, likewise, acquired work through the Civilian Conservation Corps (CCC), the Public Works Administration (PWA) and Works Progress Administration (WPA), while quotas, intended to ensure proportional representation, gave many African Americans access to newly constructed public housing projects in the era before public housing was a vehicle for warehousing poor people.[7] Yes, the 23 percent of agricultural and domestic workers who happened to be black were, like their white counterparts, excluded from coverage under the NLRA, the FLSA, and the SSA. But

African American industrial workers—such as the 500,000 blacks who comprised 8 percent of the Congress of Industrial Organizations' (CIO) membership in 1945[8]—were covered by each of these pieces of legislation.

There is no question that African Americans did not receive their fair share of New Deal programs—particularly in housing. But the now commonplace tendency to dismiss the Roosevelt administration's crucial role in improving the material lives of millions of African Americans has obscured both the importance of the New Deal's redistributive policies to blacks—who demonstrated their support for the administration with their votes—and the influence of New Deal liberalism over the scope of black political activism from the 1930s through the civil rights movement.

New Deal Industrial Democracy and Black Civil Rights

In 1978, historian Harvard Sitkoff's *A New Deal for Blacks* laid the foundation on which a generation of civil rights scholarship would rest. Sitkoff's ambitious study of Depression-era race relations and politics traced the origins of the modern civil rights movement to the 1930s and early 1940s. While Sitkoff was clear that African American civil rights advanced little during the New Deal, he convincingly argued that the so-called Depression decade was fertile ground for several political, social and intellectual developments that would eventually blossom into the insurgent black political activism of the 1950s and 1960s.

The Roosevelt administration's emphasis on redistributive economic policies and the presence of civil rights advocates in key positions in New Deal agencies set the stage for the era of black Democratic interest-group politics. The left-labor militancy advanced by the Communist Party's (CP) Popular Front and the CIO engendered racial liberalism among a stratum of white activists and rank-and-file unionists, opening access to good blue-collar jobs while providing African Americans useful political allies. Finally, the antifascist impulses influencing both left activism and America's support for the European Allies strengthened the hand of social scientists and liberals who challenged notions of racial hierarchy rooted in eugenics or other biological metaphors. Each of the above, according to Sitkoff, not only informed the activist sensibilities of African Americans during the Depression and World War II, they also shaped the scope of the modern civil rights movement.[9]

While *A New Deal for Blacks* offered a compelling overview of the relationship between New Deal policy and the struggle for black equality, it did not explore the complex issues shaping civil rights institutions and their leaders during the 1930s. Thus, a great many scholars have since written books on each of the various themes Sitkoff first examined in 1978. The relationship between New Deal industrial democracy and civil rights activism during the 1930s and early 1940s has been of particular interest.

The New Deal's efforts to redress the problem of under-consumption through unionization—best exemplified by the NLRA—transformed not just the workplace but American democracy. Aware of the contradictions between the Jeffersonian democratic ideal still celebrated by most Americans in the 1930s and the realities of industrial society, New Dealers sought to use government, as President Roosevelt stated, to "assist in the development of an economic declaration of rights, an economic constitutional order."[10] The right to unionize was at the center of this agenda.

Though today's neoliberals generally disparage unions as "special interests," New Dealers understood collective agitation in the workplace as a public good. Unionization enhanced consumer purchasing power and, along with entitlements, afforded dignity and security to the nation's producer classes. This industrial democratic turn in political culture and the related rights discourse would, as I will discuss, shift the focus of African American civil rights away from narrow calls for racial equality—which basically took economic inequality as a given—toward broader demands for economic justice. New Deal industrial democracy would also encourage political militancy among black activists, who came to identify mass protest as a responsibility of citizenship.

New Deal labor law had a profound impact on the scope of African American activism during the 1930s and 1940s. Black unionists were the obvious beneficiaries of the Roosevelt administration's efforts to enhance consumer purchasing power and workers' rights. In 1937, for example, the Brotherhood of Sleeping Car Porters (BSCP) became the first African American labor union to successfully negotiate a contract with a major employer. As historian Beth Bates has argued, the BSCP's success stemmed at least partly from the political acumen of the union's leadership. Facing stiff opposition from a black elite dogmatically committed to clientage/petition politics, BSCP president A. Philip Randolph and his organizers framed the porters' quest for recognition as a matter of African American civil rights. Thus, between 1925 and the start of the New Deal, the porters' union not only established a deep base of support among blacks, but the BSCP itself helped legitimate African American protest politics.[11] Still, the organizing genius of Randolph and associates notwithstanding, the BSCP owed its legal recognition to the protections afforded unions by the Norris–La Guardia Act (1932), the Railway Labor Act of 1934 and the 1935 NLRA, more commonly referred to as the Wagner Act.

The Norris–La Guardia and Wagner Acts not only played significant roles in labor disputes, they also influenced New Deal–era civil rights politics. Norris–La Guardia prevented the courts from issuing injunctions halting legitimate labor disputes, while the Wagner Act—like section 7A of the National Industrial Recovery Act (NIRA) that preceded it— enhanced workers' rights to collective bargaining.

Together, they marked a major shift in American politics and life. In the three decades or so preceding the passage of the Wagner Act—a period known as the Lochner era—not only had the Supreme Court sanctioned employers' use of intimidation and coercion to curb unions' organizing campaigns, but it had also checked the government's ability to intervene in the employer-employee relationship through the principle known as "freedom of contract." Freedom of contract presumed that an employer and an individual employee came to the negotiating table as coequals. Taylorism should have made the absurdity of this premise plain; however, it would take the economic and political turmoil precipitated by the Great Depression to challenge the Lochner era's employer-friendly conception of work and workplace regulations. Identifying collective bargaining as the most effective vehicle for bolstering workers' negotiating strength with employers for more equitable wages, the NLRA's architects—Senator Robert Wagner and his assistant, Leon Keyserling—believed that unionization was essential to stimulating consumer demand and ending the Great Depression.[12] New Deal liberals likewise argued that unions held the potential to check managerial caprice by allowing workers to bargain collectively for contracts establishing formal guidelines for hiring, termination, promotions, raises and more.

To achieve its tandem goals of establishing a sustainable model of capitalism and addressing managerial authoritarianism, the Wagner Act eliminated the "yellow-dog" contract,[13] established the closed shop and created the National Labor Relations Board (NLRB), which was responsible for mediating legitimate labor disputes.

As can be said of any institution in America, many unions—particularly in the skilled trades—were guilty of discrimination. The absence of an antidiscrimination clause from the Wagner Act thus alarmed many civil rights leaders, who feared that the closed shop would enable discriminatory unions to bar blacks from not just their collective bargaining units but the workplace itself. Nevertheless, mainstream civil rights leaders generally called for amending the NLRA rather than repealing it.

New Deal Civil Rights Activism Was Working Class

The civil rights community's support for collective bargaining signified a notable turn in African Americans' political sensibilities. As alluded to above, the protected status afforded labor unions both inspired and legitimated a new class-inflected militancy among African American civil rights activists. With black unemployment hovering around 50 percent in cities such as New York, Chicago and Baltimore in the early 1930s, African Americans began to mobilize protest campaigns aimed at expanding employment and housing opportunities. Working-class blacks participated in Communist Party–organized Unemployed Councils, taking to the streets both to demand jobs and to thwart evictions. They also organized "Don't Buy Where You Can't Work" campaigns.

The seeds of "Don't Buy Where You Can't Work" were sown in 1929, when *Chicago Whip* editor Joseph Bibb encouraged African American consumers to boycott businesses that relied on black patronage but refused to hire black employees. Bibb's call resonated with African Americans shaped by both Depression-era unemployment and the race consciousness of the New Negro movement of the 1920s. Indeed, the earliest boycotts reflected a pronounced racial nationalism. Sufi Abdul Hamid's 1932 boycott of Harlem's Koch's department store, for example, played on racial/ethnic tensions between blacks and Jews as well as color and class divisions among African Americans.

While Hamid briefly garnered the support of a small number of middle-class black leaders, including Reverend

Adam Clayton Powell Jr., his bombastic style and anti-Semitic rhetoric quickly alienated most black elites. Hamid, who had a penchant for flowing robes and turbans, was an especially theatrical and controversial figure; nevertheless, the employment aims of early "Don't Buy Where You Can't Work" protests revealed a narrow racialism that unnerved many "respectable" black leaders.[14] T. Arnold Hill of the National Urban League (NUL), for example, expressed concern as early as 1930 that these campaigns might fuel racial tensions, undermining the cause of workplace integration.[15]

The growing popularity of "Don't Buy Where You Can't Work" would eventually compel mainstream African American leaders to play active roles in the movement. As picketers benefited from both experience and a deepening pool of financial and intellectual resources, they came to frame their employment demands in accordance with New Deal labor law. In late 1933, Kiowa Costonie's Citizens Committee characterized its boycott of A&P grocery stores in Baltimore as a labor dispute. By holding itself out as a union, the Citizens Committee hoped to gain the protections against injunction afforded strikers by the Norris–La Guardia Act. The Citizens Committee failed to persuade the courts that a legitimate labor dispute existed between its membership and A&P groceries, though, both because the group represented aspirant rather than current employees and because it demanded racial proportionalism—in other words, a quota—in employment.[16] By 1938, however, the US Supreme Court's verdict in *New Negro Alliance v. Sanitary Grocery Co.* would extend protection against injunctions to "Don't Buy Where You Can't Work." The New Negro Alliance

(NNA) initiated its boycott of DC's Sanitary Grocery shops in 1936, leading the store to seek and obtain an injunction against picketers. With the aid of Howard University law professor William Hastie and sociologist E. Franklin Frazier, the New Negro Alliance eschewed calls for racial quotas in its bid for recognition as a union, focusing instead on the sociological consequences of black unemployment.

As historian Paul Moreno makes clear, the Supreme Court would ultimately rule in the NNA's favor to ensure a broad enough interpretation of Norris–La Guardia to prevent lower courts from interpreting the act too narrowly.[17] Whatever the Supreme Court's overarching aims, however, in recognizing the NNA's grievance with Sanitary Grocery Co. as a labor dispute, it legitimated such protests and set the stage for an expansion of employment boycotts.

There is little doubt that activists involved in "Don't Buy Where You Can't Work" defined their grievances as labor disputes partly for opportunistic reasons. As activist and legal scholar Pauli Murray said about *New Negro Alliance* in 1945, the highest court in the nation "raised a shield to protect the activities of minority groups in those controversies arising out of racial or religious discrimination in matters of employment, by defining those activities as labor disputes and entitled to their immunities under the Norris–LaGuardia Act."[18] So, since Norris–La Guardia and the Wagner Act identified strikes rather than civil rights protests as protected speech, African American activists had few options but to define boycott groups as unions—even if they represented prospective rather than current employees. Still, the legitimacy conferred to organized labor by New Deal labor law sparked a transformation in black politics that extended well beyond mere convenience. African Americans of the 1930s and 1940s came to see race discrimination as an outgrowth of class inequality.[19] Thus, by the early 1930s mainstream civil rights organizations such as the National Association for the Advancement of Colored People (NAACP) and NUL began to emphasize the broader advance of the American working class as key to black uplift.

Founded a year after the 1908 Springfield, Illinois, race riot, the NAACP's mission proceeded from the view that "the problem of the twentieth century was the problem of the color line." The association's direct challenges to disenfranchisement and de jure segregation resonated with African Americans of the 1910s and 1920s, many of whom had acquired greater political and economic liberties via the Great Migration.[20] By the 1930s, however, the NAACP's narrow integrationist agenda appeared to be out of touch. Though African Americans remained steadfastly opposed to disfranchisement and segregation, poverty and unemployment were the dominant issues shaping black political consciousness during the Great Depression. As a result, the NAACP witnessed a decline in interest and membership.

Hoping to revitalize the flagging civil rights group, NAACP president Joel Spingarn organized the Second Amenia Conference for spring 1933. Spingarn tasked thirty-three participants with reinterpreting the problems confronting blacks "within the larger issues facing the nation." While the conference was not without dissenters, the activists, academics and civic leaders in attendance ultimately identified interracial working-class alliances as pivotal to racial progress. The Conference proposed no specific course of action; however, one year later, the association set out to craft a prescription via the Committee on the Future Plan and Program of the NAACP.

Headed by black economist Abram L. Harris, the committee encouraged the NAACP to transform itself into a center for workers' education and agitation. Harris thus urged the association to develop courses intended to assist blacks in making sense of their place in industry while simultaneously promoting interracial solidarity. He also called upon the civil rights group to educate workers about unionization and the importance of political participation. Finally, Harris suggested that the NAACP grant more authority to local chapters, allowing locals to circumvent the board of directors and national office so that they might pursue more aggressive agendas.[21]

Institutional concerns precluded pursuit of the goals and prescriptions advised by the Amenia Conference and Harris Report respectively. Executive secretary Walter White asserted that the financial crisis made implementation of the Harris Report infeasible. The aims of the Harris Report likewise bumped up against the sensibilities of influential benefactors such as Julius Rosenwald, who were unnerved by the growing economic militancy among African Americans.[22] Thus, while Walter White hoped to reinvigorate the association by connecting with the masses, the NAACP did not institutionalize the kind of class agenda called for by Amenia and the Harris Report until the late 1930s. Instead, the association would attempt to enhance its viability in the mid-1930s through a vigorous anti-lynching campaign.

By the end of the decade, a number of political and economic developments would lead the NAACP to reconsider the value of a labor agenda. First, the association's anti-lynching campaign failed to generate the mass appeal that White had hoped for. Indeed, the NAACP faced stiff competition from civil rights organizations such as the fledgling National Negro Congress (NNC), and, for a time, even the NUL stressed a labor approach to black uplift. Second, the association's narrow focus on barriers to blacks' social and political equality had even begun to undercut the civil rights organization's attractiveness to philanthropists. According to Beth Bates, the labor-friendly Garland Fund's rejection of the NAACP's application for a $10,000 grant in 1937 made White and associates alive to the charge that the group's historic focus looked past the pressing issues of the day.[23] Third, the rise of the CIO, with its comparatively progressive racial politics, not only opened the ranks of organized labor to tens of thousands of black Americans but also created new sources of funding. Thus, by the late 1930s, contributions from black unionists and the CIO itself had begun to offset declining philanthropic support for the NAACP.

All of this—along with Joel Spingarn's death in 1939—cleared the way for the NAACP to develop a coherent labor agenda. Walter White made the NAACP's commitment to organized labor plain in 1941 when he announced the civil rights group's support for the United Auto Workers (UAW) strike at Ford's River Rouge facility. White ultimately called upon the plant's 9,000 black employees to join in common cause with white workers in pursuit of economic justice. In extending his support to the UAW, White strengthened the NAACP's relationship with organized labor, enabling the association to create the institutional ties required for a labor-oriented civil rights program.

The NAACP's commitment to black unionism only intensified during World War II, aided by the creation of the NAACP's Legal Defense Fund (LDF) in 1939.[24] Functioning as the NAACP's separate litigation arm, the LDF equipped the civil rights group to pursue the kind of aggressive legal strategy first proposed in 1934 by Howard University law professor Charles Hamilton Houston, the NAACP's first full-time lawyer. Under the leadership of Thurgood Marshall—who had partnered with Houston in 1936—the LDF embarked on an incremental legal strategy intended to establish precedents challenging race discrimination. Identifying employment discrimination as the single most important issue facing African Americans, Marshall and the LDF would litigate a number of significant workplace discrimination cases during World War II. The LDF struck major blows against discriminatory labor unions via *Steele v. Louisville & NR Co.* (1944), *Tunstall v. Brotherhood of Locomotive Firemen* (1944), and *James v. Marinship* (1944); in these cases, the NAACP argued that unions were state actors—pointing to protections afforded by the Railway Labor Act and the Wagner Act—and were thereby prohibited from denying equal protection to blacks by the Fourteenth Amendment. Though the high court rejected the more expansive definition of state actors sought by the NAACP, it did rule that the government had a compelling public interest to bar racial discrimination in unions.[25]

The association's emphasis on equal protection in the workplace was by no means a complete departure from its historic mission. As historian Risa Goluboff contends, the NAACP simply added labor to a legal agenda, centered on the Fourteenth Amendment, that already included education, transportation, housing and voting. Goluboff laments that the NAACP's emphasis on racial discrimination rather than "inequality, personal insecurity or other manifestations of racial and economic 'injustice' " reflected the continued sway of middle-class sensibilities over the group's work.[26] Still, whatever its limitations, the addition of labor to the NAACP's program reflected the leftward drift of black civil rights of the 1930s and 1940s and the related transition from clientage politics to protest activism.

The National Urban League's program in the 1930s also bore the imprint of the growing labor militancy shaping New Deal–era black politics. Founded in 1910, just a year after the NAACP, by black sociologist George Edmund Haynes, the NUL was established partly to ease rural black migrants' transition to industrial cities by addressing the material and cultural barriers to black integration. In contrast to the NAACP, the Urban League eschewed direct challenges to racist policies and practice. Proceeding from the view that blacks would only overcome whites' visceral prejudices through proper conduct, the league developed programs intended to acculturate migrants and impoverished blacks. The NUL and its locals likewise encouraged employers and landlords to provide deserving blacks access to decent jobs and housing. The group's emphasis on self-help has led some scholars to cast the league's philosophy in the conservative light of Booker T. Washington. Though the NUL was firmly imbedded in the conservative wing of the civil rights movement, the group's approach owed more to the bourgeois liberalism of the famed Chicago School of Sociology than the Wizard of Tuskegee. Chicago sociology ultimately equipped Urban Leaguers with powerful intellectual tools to counter eugenicists' claims of black racial (inherent biological) inferiority. Still, Chicago School race-relations models such as social disorganization/reorganization and ethnic cycle often led Urban Leaguers to emphasize the needs of middle-class blacks, as these individuals already possessed the cultural and intellectual attributes necessary to demonstrate the race's capacity for assimilation. The NUL's identification of respectable behavior as key to black integration likewise led it to occasionally assist employers and landlords in weeding out undesirable workers and tenants.[27]

While the Urban League's work during the 1930s continued to reflect a preoccupation with the interests of middle-class African Americans, New Deal industrial democracy would inspire the social work organization to take an activist turn. The league first began to mobilize black workers in 1933 through its Emergency Advisory Councils (EAC). The EACs set out to combat discrimination in recovery programs both by lobbying officials in the National Recovery Administration (NRA) and other New Deal agencies and by encouraging black workers to demand their fair share of relief. Blending petition and interest group politics, local EACs achieved some success in breaking down barriers to relief programs in Chicago and other cities.[28]

The NUL's efforts to mobilize black workers took a more militant direction in 1934 with the creation of the Workers' Councils (WC). The brainchild of T. Arnold Hill, longtime director of the Urban League's Department of Industrial Relations, the Workers' Councils identified collective agitation, rather than personal responsibility, as the surest route to black economic equality. Workers' Councils thus educated blacks about the implications of federal recovery efforts and labor law. WCs likewise mobilized grassroots protest campaigns, such as the 1936 campaign demanding an antidiscrimination amendment to the Wagner Act. Finally, the Workers' Councils encouraged African Americans to join in common cause with white workers in labor unions. After centralizing operations in the Workers' Bureau (WB), headed by Lester Granger, the WC spread like wildfire. At the conclusion of four years of operation, the WB established seventy Workers' Councils in twenty-one states representing tens of thousands of black workers.[29]

The bureau's calls for increased black participation in the union movement required the group to work directly with organized labor. The WB continued the NUL's longstanding efforts to encourage the American Federation of Labor (AFL) to open its ranks to African Americans.[30] Though the AFL ignored the WB's calls for racial fair play, the Urban League would find an important ally in the fledgling CIO. Founded in 1935 by United Mine Workers' president John L. Lewis, the CIO focused principally on unskilled and semiskilled laborers, who comprised the core of the nation's industrial workforce. Since most African American workers were unskilled, the democratic potential of the CIO's industrial focus was clear to the WB's Granger from the outset.

The comparative racial liberalism that characterized the CIO's organizing drives in the steel industry between 1936 and 1943 would affirm the Urban League's commitment to the industrial union. The NUL's Workers' Bureau thus not only encouraged African Americans to affiliate with CIO locals, but in 1938 the NUL would dissolve the Workers' Councils, turning over their work in support of black unionization to the CIO.[31]

The same year the NUL discontinued its Workers' Councils, Granger delivered an address to the NAACP's Youth Council that left little doubt as to the class perspective that informed the WB's work. Granger's "Challenge to the Youth" proceeded from the view that poverty and unemployment were the chief challenges confronting African Americans in the 1930s. After criticizing his own "New Negro" generation for naively presuming that individuals—in the form of respectability politics, self-help or entrepreneurialism—could successfully challenge Jim Crow and uplift the race, Granger lauded New Deal-era black youth for correctly identifying interracial workers' alliances as the key to racial equality. As Granger put it, young African Americans of the late 1930s not only understood that they must fight for "the man at the bottom," because anyone could find themselves there in modern times, but they had come to embrace the political necessity of (economic) alliances with whites. "Slowly and painfully young people are learning the Negro's fight for freedom is not a fight of the Negro for Negro freedom," Granger asserted, "but that the Negro's fight is only a small part of a nation-wide struggle—not of ten or twelve million Negroes, but of fifty-five millions of Negroes and whites, the majority of the population of this country."[32]

The fact that the Urban League developed a formal commitment to unionism several years before the more militant NAACP highlights the complex relationship between external political pressures and institutional prerogatives. The NUL—despite its comparative conservatism—was better positioned institutionally and, in some ways, philosophically to shift with the labor sensibilities of the era. Though funding constraints—the group's reliance on corporate benefactors—had prevented the league from adopting a formal union program prior to the New Deal, NUL officials such as T. Arnold Hill had advocated a labor platform since the mid-1920s. In the NUL's first two decades of operation, Urban Leaguers contended that union affiliation offered African Americans two advantages. First, unionization held the potential to enhance blacks' wages. Second, drawing from Chicago School race-relations theory, many League officials, such as Charles S. Johnson, believed that shared workplace experiences held the potential to elevate black-white relations by humanizing members of each race, thereby dispelling racial stereotypes.[33] These were, of course, among the rationales behind the league's embrace of labor militancy during the New Deal. The liberal ideology informing the Urban League's cautious, if not conservative, uplift strategy during the era of the Great Migration served, ironically perhaps, as the foundation on which the NUL's labor militancy would rest during the 1930s.

Though many scholars and civil rights activists shared the

WCs' identification of interracial unionism as a vehicle for black equality, the National Negro Congress (NNC) was perhaps the clearest institutional expression of the labor orientation of New Deal civil rights politics. Operating from 1936 to 1947, the NNC was the brainchild of John P. Davis. Davis—a graduate of Bates College and Harvard University—had begun his activist career in 1933, when he and a young Robert C. Weaver formed the Joint Committee on National Recovery (JCNR). Davis and Weaver conceived the JCNR as a civil rights lobbying group. The two men thus not only investigated violations of black civil rights in the South but drew attention to the racial limits of New Deal liberalism. In 1935, the JCNR testified before Congress on racial discrimination in NRA wage codes, the implications of the exclusion of agricultural and domestic workers from the then-pending Social Security Act and the Roosevelt administration's reluctance to press for anti-lynching and anti-poll tax legislation.[34]

Aware that effective interest group politics required mobilized constituencies, Davis called upon civil rights organizations to establish the National Negro Congress in 1935. The NNC was formed shortly thereafter, holding its first convention in February 1936. Davis, who maintained ties to both New Deal reformers and the Communist Party, modeled the National Negro Congress on the CP's Popular Front. He thus conceived of the NNC as an umbrella organization representing a broad cross section of labor activists, civil rights leaders, intellectuals and artists. This approach proved effective at the outset: the NNC's 1936 convention garnered affirmative responses from 750 delegates from twenty-eight states. Notable convention participants included political scientist Ralph Bunche—a key NNC organizer—philosopher Alain Locke, the NUL's Lester Granger and Elmer Carter, the NAACP's Roy Wilkins and the BSCP's A. Philip Randolph.[35]

Interracial unionism was at the center of the NNC's civil rights agenda. The NNC's faith in the civil rights potential of interracial working-class solidarity was, in part, a reflection of the racial liberalism taking root in the American union movement. Like the Workers' Councils, the National Negro Congress enthusiastically supported the CIO. Indeed, shortly after the NNC's first convention, John P. Davis, working directly with the CIO's John L. Lewis, placed three black organizers from the NNC's fold with the Steel Workers' Organizing Committee (SWOC). These individuals—Henry Johnson, Leonidas McDonald, Eleanor Rye—worked tirelessly to recruit blacks in SWOC's 1936 and 1937 organizing drives in mills from Chicago, Illinois, to Gary, Indiana. NNC members would likewise assist the Packinghouse Workers' Organizing Committee (PWOC) and the Tobacco Stemmers and Laborers' Union (TSLU) in their organizing drives in Chicago and Virginia respectively.[36]

The National Negro Congress's labor approach to African American civil rights likewise reflected the politics of the NNC's leadership and members. Labor unionists and leftists —Communist Party members in particular—comprised the bulk of the National Negro Congress's membership. Though left activists were generally committed to redressing both race and class inequality, leftists and labor-liberals of the era typically perceived racism as an outgrowth of class exploitation. As

A. Philip Randolph, who served as NNC president from 1936 to 1940, asserted: "no black worker can be free so long as the white worker is a slave and by the same token, no white worker is certain of security while his black brother is bound."[37] Like the JCNR that spawned it, the National Negro Congress not only fought for racial parity in the administration of New Deal programs, but it also railed against Jim Crow. Moreover, the NNC's labor activities, particularly in the South, required the group to challenge racialist sensibilities among both black and white rank-and-file unionists as well regional social conventions. Such efforts notwithstanding, the NNC's left orientation led the group to emphasize economic over social equality, as its leadership generally presumed that racism could only be eliminated by elevating the American working class irrespective of race.

The Communist Party's significance to the National Negro Congress ensured that the NNC's most important years spanned from 1936 through 1939—the era of the Popular Front. In this period, the group not only mobilized African Americans and whites to demand economic and racial equality but also organized rallies against European fascism. With the signing of the Molotov-Ribbentrop Soviet-German nonaggression pact in August 1939, however, the NNC's fortunes waned. The NNC's Communist Party members closed ranks, appearing to repudiate the antifascist politics they had embraced to that point. Dismayed by what they perceived to be the CP's unprincipled conversion, most non-Communist members bolted from the National Negro Congress. By April 1940, Randolph had resigned from the group, citing his concerns that the NNC had become a front for the CP, an organization Randolph, a Socialist Party member, had long considered suspect.[38]

Though the NNC operated until 1947—when it finally succumbed to postwar anticommunism—the group never recovered from the political infighting that prompted Randolph's departure. Despite the NNC's short history, however, many scholars contend that it left an enduring legacy. Historian Thomas J. Sugrue asserts that the NNC's antifascist campaigns established the blueprint for the kind of internationalism that would shape Cold War civil rights. The NNC's success also, as historian Beth Bates has noted, pushed mainstream civil rights organizations such as the NAACP to the left. Some have likewise suggested then that the NNC set the stage for a more activist civil rights movement, as local chapters in cities such as Chicago and New York skillfully mobilized African Americans in grassroots campaigns.

While there is little doubt that the National Negro Congress's left-wing politics distinguished it from the liberal middle-class NAACP and NUL, it is not clear that the NNC ushered in a new era in black activism. As mentioned, the NAACP had begun to consider a labor platform as early as 1933. More importantly, the labor program initiated by the NUL's Workers' Councils in 1934 overlapped the agenda begun by the NNC in 1936. Instead of transforming black politics, then, the NNC's popularity is illustrative of the wide appeal of labor activism among African Americans during the 1930s and 1940s. The NNC may therefore represent the apotheosis of the industrial democratic slant of New Deal era civil rights activism.

Black Labor Activism and Antidiscrimination Policy

By the early 1940s, the left liberalism that had shaped New Deal–era civil rights activism had culminated in a national political campaign—A. Philip Randolph's March on Washington Movement (MOWM). Several months after his resignation from the NNC, Randolph would use the protest tactics he had honed as a labor and civil rights activist to pressure President Roosevelt to redress pervasive workplace discrimination. By late 1940, the economic recovery precipitated by World War II had put a significant dent in white unemployment. African American unemployment, however, remained virtually unchanged. Racist hiring practices were largely to blame for the widening gulf between black and white workers. Indeed, a US Employment Services survey of defense contractors found that more than 50 percent of respondents refused to hire African Americans under any circumstances.[39]

In fall 1940, Randolph, NAACP executive secretary Walter White and NUL's acting executive secretary, T. Arnold Hill, met with President Roosevelt to discuss the economic crisis afflicting black Americans. Randolph would make four demands of Roosevelt. He called upon Roosevelt to bar discrimination on the part of defense contractors, federal agencies and labor unions. He also demanded that the president desegregate the armed forces. Randolph ultimately threatened to march as many as 100,000 African Americans on Washington, DC, if he did not receive a satisfactory response. Concerned that the proposed march might incite a race riot on the eve of war, Roosevelt issued Executive Order 8802 in June of 1941, barring discrimination in federal agencies and in defense employment. The Fair Employment Practices Committee (FEPC), EO8802's centerpiece, served as a compliance board.[40]

Randolph's victory cannot be attributed to the efforts of one man alone. Indeed, Randolph's proposed march functioned as a meaningful threat only because he and the BSCP leadership had created networks of organizers and sympathizers via the porters' union and the NNC. The political infrastructure established by the BSCP enabled Randolph to turn a simple threat into a movement. Though Randolph called off the march shortly after Roosevelt issued EO8802, he maintained the MOWM through late 1943 both to adopt a posture of vigilance vis-à-vis Roosevelt and to stave off African American critics who believed Randolph had not gone far enough.[41] The MOWM's popularity faded in 1943, as middle-class black leaders withdrew their already qualified support following the Detroit race riot. The MOWM had nonetheless achieved all that it could by this point.

Black unemployment declined between 1942 and 1945; however, the FEPC's contribution to this trend is unclear. Though EO8802 provided the nation's courts—in cases such as *James v. Marinship*—a wedge with which to open employment to blacks and other racial/ethnic groups, the FEPC lacked the power to enforce its own antidiscrimination guidelines. Indeed, the committee's efficacy hinged on employers' and unions' susceptibility to shame, as it relied principally on moral suasion and education to discourage workplace discrimination.

The FEPC was further hampered by President Roosevelt's questionable commitment to its work, particularly during the FEPC's first incarnation from 1941 to early 1943. Indeed, President Roosevelt greatly weakened the FEPC in 1942, when he transferred control over the committee from the Office of Price Management to the War Manpower Commission headed by Paul McNutt, an antagonist to the FEPC. In response to pressure from Randolph and other activists, President Roosevelt reorganized the FEPC again, in 1943, this time strengthening it, via Executive Order 9346.[42] In light of the constraints on the FEPC's work, the increases in black gainful employment over the course of World War II may have had more to do with wartime labor shortages than antidiscrimination policy. Still, as historian Paula Pfeffer argues, the FEPC and the threat of the march on Washington that spawned it would have a significant impact on the scope of black protest politics in decades to come.[43]

Studies of A. Philip Randolph and the BSCP have demonstrated strong continuities between the labor militancy shaping civil rights activism during the New Deal and World War II and the modern civil rights movement. Following the war, Randolph fought for integration of the armed forces, desegregation of public accommodations, voting rights legislation, and integration of craft unions. The breadth of civil rights issues with which Randolph was concerned was not simply a reflection of his own sense of social justice; it was also illustrative of the rightward drift in American politics.

McCarthyism and the related assault on organized labor had lessened the sway of working-class militancy over African American civil rights. Civil rights campaigns of the 1950s and early 1960s were thus less concerned with economic justice than social and political equality. Nevertheless, Randolph, a committed trade unionist, continued to press for economic fairness. Identifying lingering discrimination in skilled trades as an important source of black poverty, Randolph established the Negro American Labor Council (NALC) in 1959. The NALC failed to convince AFL leadership of the value of eliminating racial bars in skilled trades. Undeterred, Randolph and the NALC began organizing what would become the 1963 March on Washington.[44]

The 1963 "March on Washington for Jobs and Freedom" reflected many of the lessons Randolph learned from the March on Washington Movement of the 1940s. The march was convened by both labor and civil rights activists, including Randolph, Bayard Rustin, Martin Luther King Jr., the NAACP, the NUL, the NALC, the UAW, the Student Nonviolent Coordinating Committee (SNCC), the Congress of Racial Equality (CORE) and the Southern Christian Leadership Conference (SCLC). The rally's overarching aims reflected the lingering influence of New Deal industrial democracy. Organizers hoped to demonstrate a broad cross section of support for the Civil Rights Act of 1963 and a new permanent FEPC. They also demanded school desegregation, fair housing legislation, WPA-styled jobs programs for residents of America's declining inner cities, an increase to the federal minimum wage and a full-employment economy.[45]

Like the MOWM, the 1963 March on Washington achieved many of its desired policy outcomes, albeit in much attenuated form. The Kennedy and Johnson administrations did not accede to demands for work relief for underemployed and unemployed

African Americans; however, the Johnson administration would attempt to redress the problem of black indigence through the War on Poverty and related jobs training programs. President Johnson also worked with Congress to pass the Civil Rights Act of 1964, which would establish the legislative framework for affirmative action. Unlike the FEPC, the Civil Rights Act's compliance board, the EEOC, would eventually be endowed with the authority to compel employers and universities to comply with its antidiscrimination guidelines. The greater powers granted the EEOC notwithstanding, its origins can be traced to the FEPC. While Southern congressional Democrats killed the FEPC in 1946, more than two dozen states created their own antidiscrimination commissions between World War II and the early 1960s. As historian Paul Moreno notes, these state boards—New York's State Commission Against Discrimination (SCAD) in particular—would serve as the blueprint for the Civil Rights Act and the EEOC.[46]

The Wagner Act likewise helped lay the foundation on which antidiscrimination policy would be built. In fact, the phrase "affirmative action" first appeared in a provision in the Wagner Act that directed judges to impose financial penalties on employers who discriminated against union organizers. More to the point, antidiscrimination legislation, and the eventual implementation of affirmative action in the workplace, drew on precedent stemming from the Wagner Act.

As study after study has shown, few if any employers use quotas—which are prohibited by Title VII. Instead, employers hoping to avoid costly discrimination lawsuits established offices of equal employment to ensure compliance with antidiscrimination law. These new equal employment offices were modeled on the labor relations departments that union and nonunion firms had established in the wake of the Wagner Act. Moreover, many of the policies implemented by equal employment offices to ensure fair employment practices—including in-house grievance procedures, formal job descriptions, published guidelines for promotion and termination, salary classifications and open bidding—were already in use by labor relations departments partly because unions had demanded them. Finally, the National Labor Relations Act established a precedent, on which antidiscrimination policy would rely, for government intervention in the employer-employee relationship for the public good. Indeed, it is hard to imagine on what basis black civil rights leaders—who lobbied on behalf of a group that accounted for just 10 percent of the nation's population—would have demanded a fair employment practices act in the 1960s if the Wagner Act had not already established a precedent, in the name of the public good, for abridging the right to freedom of contract.[47]

If the labor politics of the New Deal did not catalyze the activist spirit of the modern civil rights movement, they did impart direction and, by extension, momentum to the so-called African American liberation movement. The New Deal created a legal framework, shaped by popular discontent over a decade of economic crisis, that legitimated citizens' demands on government for a more equitable and democratic society—a perspective that transcended both the labor movement and the Depression decade. Civil rights activists of the 1930s and 1940s, like most Americans of that period, embraced statist or what we might think of as social democratic curatives to the nation's economic and social ills. The labor orientation of New Deal–era black civil rights activism faded as the conservative turn in American politics following World War II reined in labor militancy, most notably by way of the Taft-Hartley Act of 1947.

The rightward drift of American politics ushered in by the Cold War ultimately led many African American activists in the postwar period to identify race prejudice as a psychological defect rather than a symptom of class exploitation. Still, black leaders remained committed to the notion, rooted in New Deal industrial democracy, that the government's proper role was to ensure "fairness" in civil society by providing some semblance of security to the citizenry. The New Deal was indeed, as Harvard Sitkoff asserted in 1978, a time for planting but not harvesting black civil rights. But for poor and working-class blacks, the harvest of Cold War–era civil rights politics was far less bountiful than it might have been had political and academic discourse on race and inequality remained rooted in political economy.

2

OSCAR HANDLIN AND THE CONSERVATIVE IMPLICATIONS OF POSTWAR ETHNIC IDENTITARIANISM

In his two terms as president, Barack Obama's best efforts to position himself as a healer of racial wounds did little to either redress racial disparities or stave off a racialized conservative backlash. Disillusioned with Obama's so-called postracial presidency, a stratum of activists and self-identified progressives would tighten their embrace of identitarian conceptions of inequality—attributing lingering disparities, at least in part, to the failure of Obama, and liberal policymakers more broadly, to acknowledge racism's durability and enduring influence over American life.

While President Obama's postracial vision may have diminished *racism's* contributions to contemporary disparities, it did not—as I will discuss in Chapter 4—deny the role of *race* in American life. Instead, the nation's first black president's postracialism shifted the blame for contemporary inequities away from both neoliberal economic policies and racism to the alleged cultural deficiencies of the black and brown poor themselves. Far from evidencing liberals' class reductionist dispositions, Obama's "postracial" presidency, its moniker notwithstanding, was actually in step with a long-standing race reductionist tendency among liberal academics and policymakers.

Although liberals have tended to coalesce around culturalist interpretations of racial inequality since the Cold War, the absence of materialist frameworks from mainstream Democratic and even contemporary academic discourse has prevented many activists and self-identified progressives from recognizing this fact. Constructs like underclass ideology, diversity and even intersectionality have helped to displace class-based analyses of race and inequality by reifying culture— uncoupling social relations from their proximate environmental influences.

Underclass ideology roots poverty in the alleged cultural deficiencies of the poor; diversity-centered calls for access to employment and educational opportunities presume that members of underrepresented groups possess unique cultural traits that might add value to the workplace or classroom;[1] and intersectional political analyses often presume that politics are informed by discrete identity-group affinities that operate independently of material circumstances.[2] Thus, for a number of decades now, political economy's influence over disparities or even interest group politics has been of diminishing concern to liberals, aided by a robust discourse centered on culture and group identity.

In the wake of the Obama presidency, the long retreat from materialist analytical frameworks in popular political discourse would contribute to a resurgence of putatively progressive, cultural-nationalist-informed political movements. Ta-Nehisi Coates's case for reparations for descendants of American slavery is perhaps the clearest expression of that tendency, insofar as the project is not only hostile to political-economic interpretations of racial inequality but proceeds from the view that racial/ethnic identities are the engine of American history and, by extension, contemporary politics.[3] According to political scientist Cedric Johnson, Black Lives Matter (BLM) suffers a similar problem. Although Johnson finds many of BLM's goals laudable, he contends that the movement's commitment to a "black exceptionalist" interpretive framework has led it to look past the carceral state's political-economic foundation. Even as BLM's "Vision for Black Lives" laid out what Johnson concedes is "an impressive platform of progressive ends" that would surely make for a more just and democratic society, he ultimately contends that this project proceeds from the erroneous assumption that "ethnic affinity," rather than coalitions based on shared material interest, is a viable basis for building the kind of broad political coalition needed to realize its ambitious legislative agenda.[4]

Informed by what Johnson has called a "Black Power nostalgia," many progressives seem to presume that the current push for ethnic-group political mobilization is a radical departure from a tired liberal playbook that has ignored race and the importance of racial group identity. In reality, however, postwar liberals were very much invested in ethnic group culture and its supposed impact on group life and American politics. In fact, as the following discussion of Oscar Handlin and the

Black Power movement will explore, postwar liberals not only reflexively divorced racial inequities from political economy but also self-consciously moved race/ethnicity to the center of discourse on inequality. For poor and even working-class blacks, the consequences of this move would be far from positive. In fact, modern liberalism's emphasis on group culture would ensure that African Americans would not receive their fair share of the fruits of the American welfare state, setting the stage for many of the disparities that animate progressives today.

Ethnic Pluralism and Postwar Liberalism

As the nation grappled with African American civil rights in the 1950s and 1960s, historian Oscar Handlin set out to make sense of the role of race in American democracy and to determine the proper path of black equality. A Pulitzer Prize–winning historian of immigration, Handlin viewed both civil rights and the experiences of American blacks through a lens of ethnic pluralism. Like many historians and social scientists following World War II, Handlin rejected race as an analytical category, asserting in *Race and Nationality in American Life* (1957) "that there is no evidence of any inborn differences of temperament, personality, character, or intelligence among the races." Instead, he argued that ethnicity—population groupings based on shared values, norms and experiences rather than biology—was "the only meaningful basis on which one can compare social and cultural traits."[5]

Handlin's identification of African Americans as an ethnic rather than racial group would ultimately lead him to draw fairly optimistic conclusions about the future of American "race relations." In 1959, for example, Handlin's *The Newcomers* assessed the character and consequences of Puerto Rican and black migration to New York City. The study, which was commissioned by the nonprofit Regional Plan Association Inc. of the greater New York metropolitan area,[6] rejected the charge that these groups were uniquely prone to social ills such as crime, vice and family dissolution. Instead, Handlin argued that many of the problems associated with African Americans and Puerto Ricans paralleled those of previous immigrant groups—the Irish, the Germans and the "New Immigrants." Blacks and Puerto Ricans, Handlin claimed, were therefore likely to follow a path toward acculturation similar to that taken by white ethnics provided the nation continued along the road to racial equality.[7]

Handlin did not invent ethnic pluralism, which was first articulated by philosopher Horace Kallen in the 1910s. But the prolific immigration historian and acclaimed public intellectual would play an important part in popularizing the framework. Indeed, Handlin's identification of ethnic groups as the basis of American society resonated with white liberals in the postwar period for a number of reasons.

First, ethnic pluralism explicitly rejected the race science that had informed Nazi genocide. Even before the conclusion of World War II, Nazism galvanized a swell of white liberal opposition to racism in the United States. The Nazis' eugenics-fueled, expansionist war of annihilation effectively burned away the veneer of respectability that "scientific racism" had attained during the interwar period. Thus, by the mid-1940s, white liberals—who, with notable exceptions, had been little concerned about racism during the interwar period—would begin to identify racial inequality as one of the major problems confronting the United States.[8]

Second, Handlin's ethnic pluralism offered a framework that harmonized with postwar liberals' disregard for political-economic interpretations of inequality. While New Deal–era Communists, socialists and labor-liberals situated both racism and racial discrimination within a larger context of capitalist labor and social relations, white liberals during and following World War II tended to treat racial inequality as a moral dilemma. In other words, liberals came to see racism—the belief in immutable biological group hierarchies—as contradictory to the nation's fundamental commitment to the basic equality of individuals. This disposition would only intensify during the Cold War, as policymakers bound their opposition to racism to a human rights discourse that rejected economic security—the right to a job, a living wage, health care and so on—as a right that should be guaranteed to citizens of so-called civilized nations and, instead, identified values consistent with liberal capitalism—the right to personal expression, private property, religious freedom—as universal rights.[9]

The right wing's assault on the New Deal's industrial democratic framework further contributed to postwar liberals' rejection of class-based critiques of racial inequality. The Taft-Hartley Act (1947) and the House Un-American Activities Committee (HUAC) would successfully check the labor movement's growth and undercut its political influence in the postwar period. Specifically, the Taft-Hartley Act's containment of the union movement—the act both curtailed organized labor's growth by region and economic sector, and restricted unions' political contributions—and Taft-Hartley and HUAC's combined attack on Communist and left unionists not only stymied labor militancy but also muzzled, even if they did not mute, an important left-wing voice in civil rights politics.

If Taft-Hartley and HUAC were "the big stick" that derailed labor militancy in the postwar era, liberal policymakers' tightening embrace of growth politics as their preferred model of managing capitalism would ultimately produce "the carrot." Indeed, the Housing Act of 1949 and the Highway Act of 1956—which expanded the market for state-subsidized homeownership into the suburbs—would do their part to demobilize the labor movement by encouraging members of a once-militant US union movement to identify as property holders and consumers.[10]

Handlin's conceptualization of the role of ethnic group culture in American life simultaneously challenged race-based and class-based assessments of inequality. In "Group Life within the American Pattern" (1949), for example, Handlin made clear that not only did he reject the concept of biological race, but he believed the ethnic group was the cornerstone of a "free society." Specifically, Handlin argued that American democracy's strength was owed largely to the plurality of associations that served its diverse citizenry. Institutions ranging from family to voluntary associations provided Americans with material support and psychological comfort, while affording individuals some insulation from the excesses of the state.

According to Handlin, ethnic culture—defined, again, as a population's shared values and norms—influenced the form and strength of a given group's institutional life. Contending that family, organized religion, and professional and benevolent associations ultimately influenced the temperaments, occupations and political behavior of individuals, Handlin would argue that the nation's diverse ethnic groups had been indispensable to the creativity, ingenuity and adventurous spirit that had made America a great democratic society.[11]

Handlin thus explicitly rejected scientific racists' and xenophobes' contention that ethnic identities were either pathological or antagonistic to American values, arguing instead that the nation's disparate ethnic groups constituted a long unrecognized asset. At the same time, his characterization of the importance of diverse ethnic cultures to national integrity diminished the state's role in influencing the material lives of its citizens. Indeed, ethnic groups rose and fell, in his view, on the strength of their cultural attributes and the institutions that regulated individual behavior. The opportunities and pitfalls produced by the political-economic landscape of the moment—say, whether one worked in a factory during the Lochner era rather than the high point of industrial democracy—were not of particular concern to Handlin.

The relationship between Handlin's formal rejection of biological race and his antagonism toward class-based analyses of inequality—bound, as it was, to a groupist worldview—revealed a fundamental problem with ethnic pluralism itself. Specifically, ethnic pluralism's emphasis on group identity generally understated the dynamic function of culture and the related fluidity of racial/ethnic identity. In other words, ethnic pluralism—much like contemporary diversity discourse—reified group identities, as Handlin and other postwar pluralists would equate ethnic identity with political interest groups.

Since today the two major parties, pollsters, certain types of social scientists and many who identify as liberals or progressives reflexively treat identity categories as political interest groups, the problems with the tendency may not be readily apparent to some. But Handlin's mystification of group culture and his commitment to identitarian rather than political-economic interpretative frameworks would lead him to a number of erroneous and often reactionary conclusions about the civil rights movement, the sources of racial inequality, and white racism that would not only find striking corollaries in the Black Power movement but should sound familiar to readers today.

Handlin's Race Reductionist Views on Inequality and Civil Rights

Between the late 1950s and middle 1960s, Handlin authored a number of critical reflections on the growing militancy taking hold of the civil rights movement. Though he believed that efforts to dismantle the South's Jim Crow regime represented the fulfillment of America's democratic ideals, he was circumspect about the movement's turn, in the 1960s, toward the northern United States and the related assault on de facto segregation. Handlin was particularly exercised over civil rights activists' pursuit of what he described as policies intended to engineer "integration"—which he defined as efforts to ensure equal outcomes—rather than "desegregation."[12]

According to Handlin, demands for proportional representation posed a number of problems. Quotas and other measures intended to "force" integration in employment and housing threatened freedom of association. He warned that quotas would trigger a backlash among whites, including potential allies, thereby curtailing the political impact of civil rights. Handlin likewise contended that the focus on outcomes glossed over meaningful differences between individuals and even groups. Efforts to ensure racial parity washed away the meritocratic principles that most Americans reflexively embraced. By contrast, laws seeking to desegregate society by extending the right to "personal security, the ballot and decent schools" to blacks not only were consistent with the American creed, but also afforded African Americans the tools necessary to build strong communities and to establish themselves as constructive members of civil society.[13]

Though sensitive to the political and economic frustrations that had inspired calls for racial proportionalism, Handlin ultimately attributed demands for so-called forced integration to irresponsible black leaders who, in his view, appreciated neither the implications of such policies nor the historic underpinnings of the economic and social crises afflicting black Americans. Indeed, Handlin claimed that forced integration's appeal rested on the erroneous presumptions that blacks not only faced unique challenges, but that racism was so ingrained in American culture that statist intervention was the sole remedy.

As he had argued in *The Newcomers,* Handlin traced

contemporary problems afflicting black Americans not to slavery, as Daniel Patrick Moynihan had, but to the Great Migration. Migrants' transition from comparatively static rural communities to industrial cities characterized by fluidity and individualism undermined traditional institutions of social control, setting the stage for ills such as family dissolution and delinquency. Black migrants likewise had difficulty adjusting to the political and economic opportunities and responsibilities of urban life. All of these problems, as Handlin noted, paralleled those encountered by previous immigrant groups.[14]

The similarities between the experiences of African Americans and other ethnic groups were important to Handlin partly because they offered a blueprint for appropriate civil rights policy. Racism was a real obstacle in Handlin's view, particularly in the South. But in the absence of formal barriers to employment, housing and public accommodations, the major impediment to black mobility was, according to Handlin, African Americans themselves. Specifically, Handlin argued that blacks' late arrival to the urban North discouraged the African American leadership class from organizing the kinds of voluntary associations that had been so beneficial to white ethnics. Instead of developing their own civic groups that were capable of addressing African Americans' specific needs, blacks, Handlin claimed, turned to New Deal and other government programs for assistance. The absence of strong black civic organizations denied African Americans the kind of intragroup tutelage that Handlin believed had been pivotal to the acculturation of previous generations of ethnic immigrants.[15]

Handlin's effort to situate black migrants' experiences within a broader context of ethnic immigration and urban history was not without merit. Indeed, the immigration historian's rejection of slavery as the source of social ills afflicting black Americans in the industrial age serves as an incisive critique of Moynihan that—despite Moynihan's rehabilitation since the 1980s—is buttressed by half a century of scholarship on slavery.[16] Still, Handlin's framework suffers from a number of significant problems.

First, Handlin's characterization of blacks as the "last immigrants" was simply wrong. African Americans had lived in northern cities even before the nation's founding. And though there is no doubt that white ethnics, such as the so-called New Immigrants, faced what is rightly understood as racial discrimination in the early twentieth century, social scientists like W.E.B. Du Bois, Charles S. Johnson and E. Franklin Frazier had long made clear that African American migrants faced far stiffer opposition to workplace and neighborhood integration than their white ethnic counterparts.

Second, Handlin's assessment of pre–New Deal black civic leadership was also incorrect. In fact, northern blacks had begun to develop organizations intended to acculturate African American migrants to "middle-class norms" even before the Great Migration. The NUL, for example, established in 1910, had crafted a racial uplift strategy that paralleled the Americanization projects pursued by white ethnic groups.[17] Influenced by models of assimilation pioneered by the Chicago School of Sociology, the NUL traced the social ills associated with migration to a collective alienation arising from black migrants' transition from gemeinschaft to gesellschaft. The Urban League, therefore, set out to facilitate African American migrants' adjustment to the industrial city by addressing the very problems of social disorganization with which Handlin was concerned.[18] To be sure, black civil rights groups such as the NUL and NAACP would turn to the federal government for assistance by the New Deal; however, they and scores of other voluntarist associations of the era looked to the government partly because the challenges posed by the Great Depression far exceeded the capabilities of charitable organizations.[19]

Third, and this is the fundamental issue, Handlin's characterization of "integrationist" policies revealed ethnic pluralism's essentialist bent, as well as Handlin's related disregard for the New Deal and postwar welfare states' crucial role in shaping material outcomes for both whites—ethnic or otherwise—and blacks. While Handlin formally rejected the notion that the so-called races were biologically distinct, he nonetheless believed that ethnic/racial groups maintained particular cultural identities that warranted policymakers' attention. Specifically, Handlin presumed that ethnic groups maintained a "cultural" essence that transcended either material circumstances or proximate environmental influences. This is why he believed that ethnic voluntarist groups were better suited than government both to mentor their unacculturated brethren and to represent them as coherent interest groups. A major problem with "forced integration," then, was that such efforts obliterated cultural distinctiveness.

Ethnic Pluralism's Conservative Implications

Handlin's essentialist framework would not only lead him to understate or even ignore the influence of political, economic and regional diversity over "black identity," but it would also lead him to overstate race/ethnicity's efficacy as an organizing tool. *Successful* civil rights campaigns—the March on Washington Movement of the 1940s, the Montgomery Bus Boycott (1955–6), the Prayer Pilgrimage for Freedom (1957), the lunch counter sit-ins (1960), the 1963 March on Washington for Jobs and Freedom, the Selma March (1965) and so on—all coalesced around specific policy aims rather than amorphous racial identity. And, of course, the modern civil rights movement's judicial and legislative successes required a broad inter-racial base of support.

More to the point, the centrality of ethnic identity to Handlin's analysis caused him to frequently look past the impact of housing and economic policy on what we generally refer to as racial disparities. This would, ironically, lead Handlin to rationalize de facto segregation via reification of the prejudices that informed it. In "The Goals of Integration," for example, Handlin argued that because de jure segregation in education was *intended* to buttress the South's system of racial hierarchy, *Brown v. the Board of Education* was warranted—although he rejected the notion that segregation inflicted psychological damage on blacks and whites. By contrast, Handlin claimed that segregation in education in the North was emblematic of residential patterns, rather than policies intended to disadvantage blacks, and therefore merited no meaningful intervention.

While he was clear that racial/ethnic patterns were evident in residential neighborhoods, Handlin asserted that such demographic trends arose organically from residents' desires to establish communities of their own making. To be sure, Handlin conceded that race prejudice was often a facet of this process. Still, the core issue, he claimed, was the middle class's basic desire to maintain a distinct communal life. Demands for housing integration thus not only ran afoul of community, but they missed the mark. Blacks, Handlin contended, needed quality housing in their own communities.[20]

While Handlin's *The Newcomers* had offered a more nuanced account of housing discrimination that acknowledged the impact of race prejudice on housing markets, his analysis here, too, was wed to the view that black progress hinged not on state intervention but racial self-help. Specifically, Handlin identified black entrepreneurialism as key to opening housing opportunities to blacks. The success of ventures like the African American–owned Carver Savings and Loans, he argued, held the potential to demonstrate the profitability of black home-ownership. Handlin likewise suggested that African Americans were themselves to blame for their low rates of homeownership insofar as too many, he argued, were reluctant to enter new housing markets for fear of conflict. Group-specific uplift was therefore pivotal to black progress.[21]

Handlin's characterization of neighborhood formation as an organic process was, of course, far removed from reality. As subsequent generations of urbanists have shown, residential segregation was the product not simply of personal predilection but of policy. Suburbanization and the related concentration of blacks in cities in the throes of deindustrialization was fueled, in large part, by FHA and Veterans Administration (VA) mortgage policy, which excluded African Americans from eligibility for long-term mortgages until the late 1960s. Urban renewal—the product of the Housing Act of 1949—likewise razed even vibrant black communities in pursuit of business-oriented pro-growth policies, further ghettoizing African Americans in moribund central cities by housing a large share of the dislocated in apartment projects.

Even the notions of community integrity that Handlin held as sacrosanct were contrived by the alliance between government and the real estate and banking industries. Indeed, realtors, housing economists and planners had constructed racialized notions of homeownership and community as justification for restrictive covenants as early as the 1910s and 1920s. During the era of FHA mortgages, the relationship between race and community had become federal policy as the presence of blacks and other undesirables formally threatened neighborhood integrity and, by extension, property values.[22] So, while the language of homeownership may have centered on community cohesion and market imperatives, the concept of community was hardly race-neutral.

None of this is to suggest that Handlin completely ignored the relationship between policy and group identity. Indeed, Handlin's critique of affirmative action in the workplace presumed that quotas would construct *artificial* group identities. As Handlin asserted in 1966, "demands for preferential hiring, for assigned quotas of desirable jobs, and for a Black Man's Marshall Plan are sometimes presented as if they were the means of attaining racial balance and therefore of furthering integration." According to Handlin, however, such demands actually called "for recognition of the special character of the group; and to the extent that they are heeded, they strengthen this identity." Handlin claimed that racial proportionalism would do little to elevate blacks' economic standing because, as mentioned above, he believed that African Americans' marginality stemmed largely from their late arrival to northern cities and related failure to create their own voluntarist associations. Though Handlin conceded that the majority of black workers had been confined to unskilled and poorly paid occupations, he argued that race was not the sole culprit; family influences and other environmental factors shaped an individual's occupational choices.[23] Handlin would stake out a similar position on affirmative action in his 1994 *Liberty and Equality*, where he and his wife, Lilian Handlin, argued that affirmative action blurred lines of socioeconomic distinction among blacks and created a group mentality that identified preferential treatment as a right.[24]

While Handlin cast the ethnic political identities engendered by affirmative action as inauthentic, such constructs were no less organic than notions of community fostered by homeownership—a matter that Handlin's ethnic pluralist framework did not permit him to see. Handlin's reification of ethnic communities likewise led him to look past the intimate relationship between race and other environmental factors, such as family connections, that shaped an individual's economic prospects. The combination of workplace and housing discrimination limited African Americans' access to skilled trades and professions, allowing only a select minority to pass on connections or meaningful skills—both technical and soft—to their offspring. As social scientists ranging from Mercer Sullivan to William J. Wilson have shown, racial discrimination and its legacy helped to limit the social capital of the disadvantaged.

Worse yet, Handlin's critique of affirmative action failed to give serious consideration to either the scope of blacks' demands for economic opportunity or the history of anti-discrimination policy over the two decades preceding the 1964 Civil Rights Act. Indeed, civil rights activists' calls for proactive antidiscrimination measures were shaped, in part, by experiences with state-level fair employment practices commissions. The nondiscrimination guidelines issued by state antidiscrimination agencies, which were essentially outgrowths of the World War II–era federal FEPC, had initially focused on disparate treatment (an employer's explicit refusal to hire blacks and other groups) rather than disparate impact (the consequences of managerial practices on the composition of the workforce). By the early 1960s, civil rights leaders and many policymakers knew all too well that simply outlawing explicit racial bars in employment would not necessarily end discriminatory employment practices.[25]

Handlin's contention that affirmative action was incapable of fully redressing black poverty was correct, though not for the reasons he identified.[26] Nevertheless, demands for either proportional representation or proactive recruitment of minority workers and students (which is actually what affirmative action is, not quotas) were, on their own terms, neither irrational nor ignorant. Experience with what Handlin would describe as policies intended to bring about "desegregation," along with political expediency, ultimately influenced black workers, activists and liberal policymakers' pursuit of racial parity, whatever its limitations.[27]

Moreover, while most civil rights leaders of the 1960s rightly embraced the necessity of both antidiscrimination legislation and minority recruitment programs, the decade's most ambitious call for a "domestic Marshall plan"— A. Philip Randolph and Bayard Rustin's "Freedom Budget for All"—was not intended to benefit African Americans exclusively, precisely because Randolph and Rustin, in contrast to Handlin, traced racial disparities to economic processes that transcended ethnicity and race. To be sure, the Black Power movement—which gained prominence at the very moment Randolph and Rustin proposed their Freedom Budget—would "call for recognition of the special character of [African Americans]" and the challenges they faced. But, as I will discuss below, Black Power's political project—which, like Handlin, presumed that ethnic-group identity and self-help were key elements of American democracy—was influenced, ironically, by ethnic pluralism.

Handlin's identification of ethnic culture as the engine of socioeconomic mobility draws attention to the conservative implications of ethnic pluralism. While the culturalist framework formally departed from notions of biological determinism that drove American race relations from the late nineteenth century through the 1930s, ethnic pluralism failed to break fully from notions of group distinctiveness. Indeed, Handlin's assessment of the civil rights movement revealed a tendency to view black protest politics through the lens of tribalism rather than power. Though he was clear that race discrimination was a significant obstacle to African American civil rights, Handlin nonetheless believed that desegregation required that blacks *earn* equality through cultural development. This, as I have discussed, would prompt Handlin to dismiss calls for "integration" as artificial forcing. It would likewise lead him to arbitrarily distinguish between black *ethnic* and *political* identities—as revealed by his response to calls for affirmative action—with Handlin casting the latter as inauthentic.

Handlin's culturalist framework was illustrative of the triumph of Boasian anthropology and Chicago School race-relations theory over eugenics—a victory cemented by the horrors of Nazism. Still, the pluralist turn in the social sciences and history following World War II would simply substitute cultural hierarchy for biological determinism. As literary theorist Walter Benn Michaels has shown, as early as the late 1910s, pluralists' discussions of national character and ethnic identity presumed that groups maintained a cultural integrity that transcended proximate environmental influences. So, while culture was a more malleable concept than heredity, in the age of the affluent society, cultural hierarchy functioned to explain inequality by looking past its structural and political origins. Indeed, the ambiguous relationship between culture and environment that Michaels points to diminished the analytical importance of economic class to pluralists during the Cold War.[28] Thus, by the 1960s, liberals rarely described racism or even poverty as products of class exploitation, in contrast to liberal analysis during the New Deal and World War II. Instead, pluralists—such as Oscar Handlin, Daniel

Patrick Moynihan and Nathan Glazer—traced the origins of such ills to the cultural deficiencies of the disadvantaged and the attitudes of the privileged.

The Problem with Ethnic Pluralism for Black Politics

Ethnic pluralism's sway over postwar liberal academics and policymakers ensured its influence over African American political thought. Ta-Nehisi Coates and a long list of liberal and conservative Moynihan apologists have attributed the Great Society's failure to eliminate racial inequality to the Johnson administration's rejection of assistant secretary of labor Daniel Patrick Moynihan's ethnic pluralist interpretation of black poverty. However, as I discuss in Chapter 3, the War on Poverty's inadequate response to racial disparities in employment and income was owed, in no small part, to the Johnson administration's commitment to the distinctiveness of African American poverty and culture. The ethnic pluralist framework that contributed to the War on Poverty's failure to close the material divide between blacks and whites would also contribute to a conservative, culturalist turn in African American politics in the form of the Black Power movement.

While the Johnson administration's insistence that "Negro poverty was not white poverty" led it to overlook the political-economic underpinnings of racial disparities, the War on Poverty would establish a bureaucratic network—encompassing federal agencies, nonprofits, neighborhood groups, social service agencies and eventually local government—that not only provided employment for an aspirant class of black government functionaries, but it would also pave the way for a wave of African American elected officials. As Cedric Johnson has argued, Community Action Programs' (CAP's) "maximum feasible participation"—which set out to bridge the divide between administrators and recipients of federal assistance—ultimately "functioned as a form of ethnic empowerment that eventually enabled [black] constituencies to wrest control of white-ethnic dominated governments" in a number of cities from the 1960s through the 1970s. CAP's commitment to maximum feasible participation thus helped black constituencies attain some influence over government services and patronage. But as Johnson writes, the War on Poverty's emphasis on ethnic group culture would also help displace "working class-centered politics by institutionalizing the view that racial identity and political constituencies were synonymous."[29]

Liberal policymakers' equation of race and ethnicity with political interest groups both meshed with and nurtured the Black Power movement. While black studies' cultural turn has led many scholars, such as Peniel Joseph, to take Black Power's militant expressions of racial-group pride and solidarity as evidence of the movement's political radicalism, this narrow focus has obscured Black Power's conservative, reformist thrust.

To be sure, the Black Panther Party's (BPP) revolutionary socialism represented a radical strain of Black Power; however, police state repression and the group's own rhetorical excesses limited the BPP's *political* influence—even if the Panthers have become synonymous with Black Power in the popular imagination. Rather than challenging the capitalist roots of material inequities, then, the Black Power movement ultimately represented a kind of petit bourgeois ethnic-group clientelist politics, which—like Handlin and, more importantly, War on Poverty programs such as CAP, Volunteers in Service to America (VISTA) and Job Corps—identified ethnic group culture as the engine of economic progress and ignored the implications of the transformation of the US economy for African Americans.[30]

Stokely Carmichael—who is generally credited with popularizing the slogan "black power"—and Charles Hamilton's *Black Power: The Politics of Liberation* (1967) offered one of the clearest expressions of ethnic pluralism's sway over the Black Power movement when they explicitly stated that Black Power proceeded from the view that ethnicity was the "basis of American politics." Before a group could "enter the open society," they asserted, "it had to first close ranks." Therefore, according to Carmichael and Hamilton, if blacks hoped to advance in the United States, African Americans would have to run *their own* organizations—asserting that "only black people can convey the revolutionary idea" that blacks are capable of self-determination.[31]

Carmichael and Hamilton's vision for Black Power was hardly a blueprint for revolutionary change. The authors simply called for reorienting the institutions that served African American communities to ensure that elected officials, public servants, administrators of federal largess and even business people "looked like" their constituents, clients and customers, because they—much like Handlin—presumed that shared ethnic identity equated with common material interest. And while—unlike Handlin—Carmichael and Hamilton presumed that the obstacles blacks faced were distinct enough from those encountered by white ethnics to merit targeted state intervention, their vision of Black Power was, as Dean Robinson has argued, much more closely aligned with postwar liberal political scientist Robert Dahl's model of ethnic group succession than the BPP's Maoism. Indeed, Carmichael and Hamilton plainly stated that African Americans needed to follow in the footsteps of other ethnic groups. As they put it, "each new ethnic group" in the United States had "found the route to social and political viability through the organization of its own institutions with which to represent its needs within the larger society."[32]

Black Power's fundamental goal, then, according to Carmichael and Hamilton, was not separatism but "community control." As they saw it, "group solidarity [was a] necessary" precondition "before a group [could] operate effectively from a bargaining position of strength in a pluralistic society."[33]

The conservative implications of Black Power's ethnic pluralist framework were plain to many contemporary left critics. Bayard Rustin—a critic of both Black Power and the War on Poverty—argued, in 1966, that the growing tide of cultural nationalism aided and abetted an anemic War on Poverty. According to Rustin, Black Power's embrace of ethnic group succession diminished both the government's and the union movement's indispensable contributions to white ethnics' ascendancy from tenements to suburbs. In other words, black cultural nationalists' tendency to attribute white ethnics' economic mobility to group culture rather than, say, the NLRA and the FHA not only was wrong but also validated the War on Poverty's rejection of the kind of interventionist policies that had in fact improved the material lives of millions of disproportionately white workers since the New Deal.

As Rustin put it, "proponents of 'black power'—accepting a historical myth perpetuated by moderates—like to say that the Irish and the Jews and the Italians, by sticking together and demanding their share, finally won enough power to overcome their initial disabilities." But "no group in American society," Rustin bluntly stated, had pulled itself up by its bootstraps. Instead, Irish Americans, Italian Americans and Jewish Americans gained political and economic power through multi-ethnic, class-based political alliances and trade union membership.[34]

Rustin warned that Black Power's emphasis on racial group representation would ultimately serve the interests of an aspirant African American political and managerial class at the expense of the vast majority of poor and working-class blacks. He was not wrong. Indeed, Black Powerites' calls for racial solidarity and economic self-determination led many to advocate what were, even in the 1960s, retrograde models of entrepreneurial uplift, which—perhaps mistaking postwar Fordism as proof that capitalism *necessarily* functioned to generate wealth for both the masses of workers and the minority of owners—would dovetail with President Nixon's promotion of "black capitalism" and, eventually, neoliberalism's equation of entrepreneurialism with freedom and its related anti-unionism.

Black Powerites' insistence that ethnic culture was the engine of group progress would likewise lead many cultural nationalists to trace African American poverty to a combination of white racism and black cultural dysfunction—also known as the "culture of poverty" or the "ghetto underclass" thesis—a framework that would ultimately serve to justify welfare reform, mass incarceration and the privatization of public services, from housing to schools.[35]

Though Rustin was clear that racism merited antidiscrimination policies, he argued that automation and the deindustrialization of American cities, not white supremacy, were the principal causes of the material divide between African Americans and whites. In other words, the problem was not that the New Deal or even racism had stalled black upward mobility by discouraging African Americans from establishing *their own* institutions, as ethnic pluralists like Handlin and Carmichael claimed. Rather, discriminatory employers, unions and public policy had denied African Americans the *full benefits* of the New Deal and postwar welfare states that had facilitated the rise of the union movement and, by extension, the rapid growth of the white American middle class since about 1940.

By the mid-1950s, however, the union movement had plateaued and industrial employment was already in decline. Rustin, therefore, insisted that race-specific remedies *alone* were incapable of redressing racial disparities. Instead, he, Randolph and economist Leon Keyserling proposed the "Freedom Budget for All," which—like the failed Full Employment Bill of 1945—would have mandated a living wage and guaranteed public-sector employment to the nation's unemployed, whatever their race.[36]

Randolph and Rustin's Freedom Budget had initially garnered wide support among civil rights leaders and left-liberals, but it would not come to pass. Its failure was not owed to an inexorable white racism. But, as I will discuss in the next chapter, the Freedom Budget's demise can be traced to postwar liberalism's retreat from political-economic understandings of inequality and the related appeal of race-reductionist frameworks like ethnic pluralism and, of course, the culture of poverty.

3

THE TRAGEDY OF THE MOYNIHAN REPORT

The Negro Family: The Case for National Action (the 1965 Moynihan Report) is perhaps the most controversial and influential non-peer-reviewed study of black poverty (or any other subject) published in the last fifty or so years. Its author, assistant secretary of labor Daniel Patrick Moynihan, was an ambitious, gregarious, liberal academic who was impressed with the civil rights movement and the legislation it helped spawn—notably, the Civil Rights and Economic Opportunities Acts of 1964. According to historian James T. Patterson, Moynihan wanted "to start a serious conversation among policymakers and to devise far reaching socioeconomic reforms." He thus aimed his study—which was printed as an in-house document—at top administration officials, with the hope that it would help them understand the devastation poverty and unemployment wrought on black families.[1]

The Negro Family ultimately caught the attention of President Johnson, who was so impressed with what he had heard about Moynihan's study that he enlisted the assistant secretary of labor to draft Johnson's Howard University address in June 1965. Not long after, news of the so-called Moynihan Report was leaked to the press. Patterson contends that early accounts of the Moynihan Report—in particular, *Newsweek*'s coverage —misrepresented the content and intent of the study. Worse yet, *The Negro Family* was formally released shortly after the August 1965 Watts Riot, which ensured that the document, focused as it was on the disintegration of black communal life, would be heavily scrutinized.[2]

The critical response to the Moynihan Report has been nearly as infamous as the document was when it was first published more than fifty years ago. Critics were especially alarmed by Moynihan's allegations of rampant social pathology among poor blacks—which, he claimed, manifested in unusually high rates of out-of-wedlock pregnancies, female-headed households and welfare dependency—as well as his ambivalence about whether the dysfunction he reported was the product of *structural* inequities or the *cultural* deficiencies of the African American poor themselves. Critics such as Carol Stack took exception to Moynihan's equation of female-headed households with social disorganization, arguing that such arrangements were less pathological than adaptive.[3] Others, among them Laura Carper and Herbert Gans, called into question Moynihan's interpretation of the data, particularly his contention that rising nonwhite AFDC caseloads revealed welfare dependency.[4] And, of course, psychologist and civil rights activist William Ryan famously accused Moynihan of "blaming the victim."

Since the 1980s, Moynihan's defenders have generally characterized him as courageous, misunderstood and visionary. In his influential *The Truly Disadvantaged* (1987), for example, sociologist William Julius Wilson described the Moynihan Report "as the only study" of its era that offered even an "abstract sense" of the long-term cumulative effects of racial inequality—"the economic and social situations into which so many disadvantaged blacks are born"—on African American family structure and culture.[5] Wilson and a long list of scholars, including Patterson, have, moreover, argued that rising rates of violent crime, female-headed households, out-of-wedlock pregnancies and welfare dependency among blacks in the decades since the publication of *The Negro Family* have vindicated Moynihan.[6] Finally, apologists have defended Moynihan against the charge of victim blaming by arguing that the Moynihan Report rooted black social pathology in "three centuries of sometimes unimaginable mistreatment" and long-term unemployment. So, while the Moynihan Report offered no concrete solutions, Moynihan believed that the problem of the Negro family would likely be resolved by a combination of jobs programs, full-employment policy and AFDC reform.

Even a cursory read of the Moynihan Report makes clear that Moynihan is not guilty of *crass* victim blaming. Indeed, as Wilson eloquently stated, Moynihan's "presentation certainly lacked elegance, but it was an attempt to synthesize structural and cultural analyses to understand the dynamics of poor black families and the plight of low-skilled black males."[7] But while Wilson proffered that statement as a defense of Moynihan, his formulation functions equally well as a critique of the Moynihan Report.

Specifically, Moynihan's efforts to synthesize a cultural and structural analysis of poverty revealed a conception of *structure* rooted not in political economy but in *ethnic pluralism*. Simply put, what Moynihan meant by structural sources of inequality was what many today would call *systemic racism* (which established barriers to black social and economic progress) and the damage that the long history of racial discrimination inflicted on the *structure of the institutions* that regulated poor African Americans' behavior and informed "black culture." To be sure, Moynihan's conception of "structural inequality" offers some insulation against the facile charge of "victim blaming"; nevertheless, Wilson's formulation ultimately highlights a more significant problem with the Moynihan Report. Moynihan was not particularly concerned about the impact of *structural economic* changes on black unemployment and poverty.

As I will discuss, Moynihan's commitment to a racialist analysis of American life numbed him to the implications, for blacks, of the US economy's structural shift from manufacturing to service and high-tech industries. Indeed, even as automation and deindustrialization had precipitated a long-run decline in the number of well-paying, low-skilled jobs that had served as white workers' pathways to the middle class since World War II—a fact noted, at the time, by secretary of labor W. Willard Wirtz, economists Charles Killingsworth and Leon Keyserling, and activists A. Philip Randolph, Bayard Rustin and Michael Harrington—*The Negro Family* and a number of Moynihan's subsequent publications downplayed the relationship between the dearth of good jobs and black poverty. Eschewing structural economic analyses of racial inequality in favor of an ethnic pluralist framework, Moynihan ultimately argued that social pathologies afflicting a stratum of poor blacks would likely undercut antipoverty initiatives that failed to account for the cultural damage inflicted upon blacks by slavery and Jim Crow.

While liberals, conservatives and even many black cultural nationalists, including Ta-Nehisi Coates, reflexively praise Moynihan for anticipating the War on Poverty's inevitable failure, the Moynihan Report's indifference to the impact of automation and deindustrialization on black life was, ironically, consistent with the perspectives of Democratic policymakers who opposed a more robust War on Poverty. Indeed, the report's emphasis on racism and black cultural pathology complemented the conservative antipoverty agenda of the Council of Economic Advisers (CEA), which—believing African American poverty to be exceptional—had identified tax cuts, antidiscrimination legislation and targeted means-tested programs rather than redistributive policies that addressed the effects of structural economic unemployment as the appropriate remedies for black poverty. The War on Poverty failed to eliminate black poverty not, as Ta-Nehisi Coates has argued, because the Johnson administration refused to recognize that "Negro poverty is not white poverty." Rather, the Johnson administration's refusal to situate African American poverty within its broader political-economic context—owed to its insistence that black poverty was exceptional—doomed the War on Poverty.

The Moynihan Report

In order to appreciate the problems with the Moynihan Report, it is necessary to discuss the document in some detail and then place it in historical context. Moynihan begins *The Negro Family: The Case for National Action* with a reflection on the implications of the recent victories of the modern civil rights movement. The passage of the 1962 Manpower and Development Training Act (MDTA), the Civil Rights Act of 1964 and the Economic Opportunity Act (1964) had fulfilled "the demand of Negro Americans for full recognition of their civil rights." Now black Americans would desire "equal results, as compared with other groups."[8]

According to Moynihan, however, two forces undermined blacks' goals. The first was "the racist virus in the American bloodstream that still afflicts all of us." The second was the toll of "three centuries of sometimes unimaginable mistreatment." The toll to which Moynihan referred was, of course, the emasculation of black men and the related disorganization of the black family. While a middle class had managed to save itself, "for the vast numbers of the unskilled, poorly educated city working class the fabric of conventional social relationships was all but disintegrated . . . So long as this situation persists," Moynihan asserted, "the cycle of poverty and disadvantage will continue to repeat itself." [9]

For Moynihan, the urban black poor were deserving of government assistance; the "tangle of pathology" that cocooned them had not yet produced the "speciation" about which he would later express concern.[10] Nevertheless, the black family was in the midst of a serious crisis: "Nearly a quarter of urban negro marriages are dissolved"; "nearly one-quarter of negro births are now illegitimate"; "almost one-fourth of negro families are headed by females." Moynihan believed that these forces culminated in "a startling increase in welfare dependency." As mentioned above, Moynihan was careful to attribute the crisis of the black family to structural forces in the form of what would eventually be termed institutional racism. He traced the origin of the matriarchal black family to slavery, which not only stripped blacks of their cultural heritage but also emasculated African American men, depriving them of their natural role as protector and provider for their women and progeny.

Emancipation conferred titular liberty; however, black men of the Jim Crow era were forced to defer in the face of public humiliation and discrimination, knowing all too well, according to Moynihan, that "the 'sassy nigger' was lynched." Urbanization and discriminatory job markets would further undermine black men and, by extension, African American family formation. Citing black sociologist E. Franklin Frazier, Moynihan suggested that migration and the destructive influences found in slums chipped away at the communal institutions that regulated social norms. Worse yet, Moynihan found that in nearly a quarter of black two-parent households, women were the principal wage earners.[11]

One implication of Moynihan's findings was a jobs program. In fact, Moynihan's analysis revealed that the number of desertions increased within twelve months of upticks in unemployment. But the Moynihan Report devotes little attention to jobs; instead, Moynihan stressed that the federal response should center on efforts that bolstered the black family and African American wage earners. Though the absence of specific recommendations is, as Patterson notes, likely illustrative of the fact that the Moynihan Report was intended as an internal document, Moynihan was actually ambivalent about the efficacy of jobs alone to solve the crisis besetting African Americans. For example, Moynihan suggested that a seemingly incongruous coincidence of a rise in nonwhite AFDC caseloads with a decline in nonwhite unemployment (1962–64) might have evinced a self-perpetuating cycle of poverty and dependency.[12] Moynihan's conclusion ultimately expressed confidence that the crisis of the black family had yet to reach the point of no return;[13] however, when he revisited this issue in "Employment, Income, and the Ordeal of the Negro Family," published shortly after the formal release of the Moynihan Report, Moynihan seemed less certain about poor blacks' prospects for escaping the "tangle of pathology."

Appearing in a special fall 1965 edition of *Daedalus*, "Employment, Income, and the Ordeal of the Negro Family" eschewed speculation about the pernicious influence of slavery on black culture and instead focused narrowly on the relationship between unemployment and family dissolution since 1930. The study thus examined issues such as blacks' shrinking footprint in agriculture; blacks' overrepresentation among blue-collar "operatives"; African Americans' increasing share of professional and clerical work; the dearth of black entrepreneurs and business managers; the income divide between blacks and whites; and blacks' "excessive dependence on the income of women."[14]

Some have suggested that his *Daedalus* article's focus leaves little doubt that Moynihan traced the crisis of the black family to joblessness. Moynihan does indeed observe a correlation between unemployment and family dissolution, leading him to declare "the cumulative result of unemployment and low income . . . has produced an unmistakable crisis in the Negro family." Still, Moynihan is explicitly ambivalent as to whether full-employment policies—which he concedes as the obvious implication of the data and "an essential first step"—would be capable of redressing the problem of social disorganization afflicting black families and communities. "An association between rising economic and social distress in the world of the Negro American," he says, "can be seen readily enough in the data, but proof of a causal relationship is a more complex matter."[15]

Reflecting again on the inverse relationship between black unemployment and nonwhite AFDC cases 1962–64, Moynihan once more suggests that the crisis in the black family may have already taken on a life of its own, divorced from jobs and unemployment. "It would be troubling indeed to learn," he said,

> that until several years ago employment opportunity made a great deal of difference in the rate of Negro dependency and family disorganization, but that situation has so deteriorated that the problem is now feeding on itself—that measures which once would have worked will henceforth not work so well, or work at all.[16]

It is worth noting the irony in Moynihan's reluctance to draw a causal relationship between black unemployment and family dissolution by the early 1960s. Though Moynihan took the inverse relationship between nonwhite AFDC caseloads and unemployment as evidence of the onset of a self-perpetuating cycle of poverty, Laura Carper observed in 1966 that the reported rise in AFDC caseloads with which Moynihan was concerned was actually the result of the liberalization of AFDC eligibility rules beginning in 1962.[17]

The Inadequacies of the War on Poverty

Moynihan's emphasis on the cultural distinctiveness of poor blacks was part and parcel of the study of poverty in the 1950s and 1960s. In the years preceding the War on Poverty, structuralists —policymakers, academics and activists alike—generally presumed that the poor possessed distinct attributes. As historian Alice O'Connor has argued, structuralists proceeded from two related observations about poverty. First, affluence rooted in economic expansion had transformed poverty from a mass phenomenon to a problem afflicting a minority of Americans. Second, poverty was largely confined to groups that were "structurally disadvantaged" by issues such as "age, geography, racial discrimination, and family income." According to structuralists, then, the very distinctiveness of the poor constituted one of the factors that placed them beyond the reach of the expanding economy. Still, even as the structuralists believed that poor people were *qualitatively* different from the middle and upper classes—which necessarily meant that unemployment and lack of income were not solely to blame for poverty—they argued that any serious antipoverty initiative had to address joblessness and/or other structural sources of economic and social inequality.[18]

Two structuralist camps emerged between the 1950s and 1960s: *economic structuralists* and *institutional structuralists*. Again, both camps generally presumed that poverty in the age of the affluent society was largely confined to out-groups—the aged, mentally or morally deficient individuals, single mothers and groups who were marginalized by geographic isolation or racial discrimination. More often than not, what distinguished the two schools was not so much their perceptions of the poor but the remedies they proposed.

Economic structuralists—such as John Kenneth Galbraith, Gunnar Myrdal and Michael Harrington—viewed poverty through the lens of political economy and thus identified redistributive programs, including public works (sometimes referred to as work relief) and job training, as the most effective weapons to combat poverty.[19] *Institutional structuralists* such as economist Oscar Ornati, by contrast, proposed policies intended to redress the character deficiencies of the poor through providing services they deemed "structurally oriented"—education, training, improvements in mental health services and so on.[20]

The contrasting perspectives of economic and institutional structuralists played out in policy debates related to black poverty in the early 1960s. Randolph's and Rustin's demands for full employment and public works via the 1963 March on Washington for Jobs and Freedom presumed that high rates of African American unemployment and poverty were the product of not just racism but deteriorating labor conditions in industries with high rates of black employment. Secretary of labor W. Willard Wirtz likewise called for public works as an essential element of any serious plan to reduce black unemployment, arguing that proportionalism in the MDTA and Area Redevelopment Act (ARA) training programs could not make a meaningful dent in black unemployment. And both Senator Joseph P. Clark's (D-PA) public hearings on fair employment practices law and Senator Hubert Humphrey's (D-MN) S-1937 (an alternative to Title VII) proceeded from much the same economic structuralist perspective.[21]

By contrast, Walter Heller and the CEA rejected the notion that redistributive policies such as public works were necessary to redress unemployment and poverty. Proceeding from the erroneous assumption that the comparatively high rates of unemployment reflected economic *cycles* rather than *shifts*, the CEA believed that short-term policies intended to stimulate growth, rather than sustained efforts intended to address fundamental changes to labor markets, were the appropriate remedy. The CEA, therefore, reasoned that a multibillion-dollar tax cut would reduce unemployment in the aggregate and engender "full employment," which was then defined as 3–4 percent unemployment.[22] Heller et al. likewise argued that tax cuts would contribute to a reduction in black unemployment, claiming that wartime stimulus had played a vital role in the economic gains African Americans had made 1940–53—a period in which black workers had actually begun to close the income and employment gap.

To be sure, CEA staffers like Robert Lampman understood that the most marginalized populations—a group that would be referred to as the "hardcore unemployed"—would be largely untouched by tax cuts.[23] Lampman thus turned to institutional structuralism to bridge the divide. In the weeks preceding the 1963 March on Washington, Lampman argued that anti-poverty measures should center on "aggressive expansionist full employment fiscal policy" combined with "anti-discrimination efforts . . . better school and public facilities for low-income children." Lampman likewise called for retraining and relocation allowances and "improv[ing] environments of the poor by community development and public housing."[24] His recommendations explicitly rejected redistributive programs altogether, casting them as not only unnecessary but counter-productive. Asserting that the poor should earn the American living standard "by their own efforts and contributions," the council claimed that "it will be far better, even if more difficult, to equip and to permit the poor of the nation to produce and to earn the additional $11 billion and more."[25]

The CEA incorporated institutional structuralism into its analysis of poverty largely to protect the tax cuts—which would benefit middle-class and upper-income Americans—from attacks from the left. Nevertheless, the CEA's adoption of institutional structuralism buttressed the appeal, as historian Carl Brauer has argued, of Community Action and other War on Poverty initiatives like Job Corps that emphasized behavioral or motivational modification rather than jobs.

Whatever Moynihan set out to do in *The Negro Family* and subsequent essays and books, his analysis of black poverty proceeded from assumptions driving *institutional* rather than *economic* structuralism. And like Heller and the CEA, Moynihan's embrace of institutional structuralism was wed to acceptance of the logic of commercial Keynesianism. In fact, Moynihan gave a nod to Heller and the CEA's stewardship of the economy in "The Professionalization of Reform" (1965). Moynihan conceded that "something called automation" was underway; however, he rejected the claim that automation was transforming American society, describing it as "simply the newest phase in a process that has been under way for at least two centuries." Moynihan believed that concerns about automation were overblown partly because, as he put it, economists had been "learning how to make an industrial economy work" since World War II.[26] Describing modern economics (of the mid-1960s) as "approaching the status of an applied science," Moynihan praised the CEA for successfully forecasting GNP and unemployment in 1964 and, of course, the related efficacy of tax-and-spend policy to stimulate growth and curb unemployment.[27]

Moynihan's characterization of the poor themselves was, as mentioned, in step with contemporaneous poverty discourse. Still, his indifference to the political-economic implications of poverty and his acceptance of the logic of commercial Keynesianism placed him in line with the CEA and the faction of policymakers who ensured that the War on Poverty would mitigate but not eliminate poverty.[28] Moynihan's observations about the black family are thus prescient only if one attributes the failures of the War on Poverty to black social pathology, sidestepping the implications of the Johnson administration's embrace of commercial Keynesianism. Indeed, the visionary status Moynihan has attained in the decades following the publication of *The Negro Family* is illustrative of the triumph of market ideology and neoliberal antistatism, as it all but ignores the fact that left-liberal economic structuralists like

Killingsworth, Harrington and Rustin anticipated the failure of the War on Poverty, arguing, in contrast to the CEA and Moynihan, that contemporary poverty was the product of automation, mechanization and deindustrialization rather than a decline in aggregate demand or a surge in social disorganization. It is worthwhile to consider what antipoverty measures would have looked like if economic structuralists had won the battle for the War on Poverty.

What a Real War on Poverty Would've Looked Like

University of Wisconsin–trained economist Charles Killingsworth, for example, was among the most trenchant left-liberal critics of the CEA-directed War on Poverty. Killingsworth—who had served as panel chairman of the National War Labor Board during World War II and chairman of the Federal Wage Stabilization Board—argued that the CEA's faith in the ability of tax cuts and antidiscrimination legislation to redress poverty proceeded from faulty if not atavistic presumptions about labor markets and a related hubris about the democratic potential of growth politics. While commercial Keynesians attributed African Americans' employment gains 1940–53 to tight labor markets engendered by wartime stimulus, Killingsworth argued that blacks' gains in this period owed more to economic intervention. Not only had conscription created an unusually tight labor market, but "demand for war goods" had, according to Killingsworth, compelled employers to transform "custom fabrication operations" into mass production facilities that subdivided "many formerly skilled jobs into simple components that could readily be taught to inexperienced, low-skilled workers." More to the point, the federal government had absorbed production costs—subsidizing recruitment and training of workers as well as machinery and plants. Unemployment plummeted during World War II (falling to an all-time low of 1.2 percent), Killingsworth claimed, thanks to a combination of wartime stimulus, a decline in the available supply of labor and government-sponsored restructuring of the economy. The employment and income gains blacks had made 1940–53 were thus not simply attributed to the expansion of the manufacturing sector but had resulted from a demand for low-skilled labor that was fostered by economic intervention.[29]

While Killingsworth acknowledged that discrimination and slack labor markets contributed to the high rates of black poverty in the mid-1960s, he observed that income and employment disparities had actually widened 1954–65—a period that witnessed the enactment of significant civil right legislation.[30] For Killingsworth, this made clear that black-white economic disparities owed less to discrimination and depressed demand than to several economic developments that hit African Americans particularly hard. First, since the mid-1950s, automation had eliminated many well-paying, low-skilled manufacturing jobs. Second, defense production had shifted from low-tech ("aircraft, ships and wheeled vehicles") to high-tech procurements ("missiles, atomic weapons, electronic equipment and other sophisticated gear"), resulting in increased demand for highly skilled workers, such as engineers and technicians, at the expense of "the low-skilled assembly-line worker." Third, the process of postwar decentralization of production meant not only that manufacturers had begun to relocate factories from the Rustbelt to the Sunbelt, but that businesses were increasingly choosing to build new stores and plants in suburbs rather than central cities. And, finally, postwar prosperity fostered a growing demand for service-sector work, which, in contrast to manufacturing, was "generally performed where customers are."[31]

Killingsworth ultimately argued that the elimination of well-paying, low-skilled manufacturing jobs via automation and deindustrialization placed most blacks—who were not only overrepresented among unskilled workers but concentrated in central cities—beyond the reach of growth politics.

For Killingsworth, then, the remedies for black unemployment were clear. Antidiscrimination measures, tax cuts and comprehensive job training programs were necessary, but insufficient. Instead, Killingsworth argued that any serious attempt to eliminate black poverty required that the government intervene directly in labor markets via public works—much as it had during the New Deal and World War II. Having "*never* seen a peacetime example of a job being redesigned for the specific purpose" of utilizing "available unskilled labor," Killingsworth insisted that a successful assault on black poverty required economic planning.[32] The absence of public works programs, in his view, ensured that low-skilled blacks in central cities would remain beyond the reach of economic stimulus.[33]

Believing that "the history of the Negroes in America—especially the history of the 1940–53 period—demonstrates that they are as ready as any group in the population to grasp opportunity when it is within their reach," Killingsworth was little concerned with the cultural implications of poverty.[34] Many other left economic structuralists, however, were invested in such matters. In "From Protest to Politics" (1965), for example, Bayard Rustin asserted, "The Negro family structure was totally destroyed by slavery and with it the possibility of cultural transmission (the right of Negroes to marry and rear children is barely a century old)."[35] In "The Politics of Poverty" (1965), white socialist Michael Harrington described black poverty as "the most terrible example of how contemporary poverty affects group psychology." According to Harrington, slavery stripped blacks "of their African heritage," abolishing "religion, the family, the tribe, or the community"; and while emancipation provided titular freedom, Jim Crow–era economic exploitation not only threatened the "the very spirit of the Negro" but emasculated "the Negro male," resulting in "a matriarchal tendency in Negro life."[36]

If Rustin and Harrington appeared to share Moynihan's sensibilities about the damage slavery and Jim Crow inflicted upon black institutional life, they were far from ambivalent about either the origins of contemporary poverty or its remedies. Indeed, Rustin and Harrington devoted only passing reference to the deleterious effects of poverty on group culture—Rustin dedicated just one sentence to the matter. Instead, like Killingsworth, Rustin and Harrington attributed high rates of black poverty to automation, mechanization and the transformation of the nation's economy from manufacturing to service-sector work—which had each contributed to the decline in the number of well-paying, low-skilled, unionized jobs that had been crucial to the expansion of the American middle class in the postwar era. In "From Protest to Politics," for example, Rustin asserted that in the late nineteenth and early twentieth centuries it was possible for a white ethnic immigrant "to start at the bottom, as an unskilled or semiskilled worker, and move up the ladder acquiring new skills along the way," particularly in the era of a burgeoning industrial unionism. By 1965, however, growth had slowed, unionization had leveled off, and America "was in the midst of a technological revolution," which, according to Rustin, altered "the fundamental structure of the labor force, destroying unskilled and semiskilled jobs—jobs in which Negroes are disproportionately concentrated."[37]

A year later, Rustin revisited this theme in "Black Power and Coalition Politics." Believing that the growing tide of cultural nationalism aided and abetted an anemic War on Poverty, Rustin insinuated that Black Powerites' embrace of ethnic group succession diminished the New Deal and postwar welfare states' indispensable contribution to white ethnics' upward mobility. As I have discussed, Rustin believed that Black Powerites' tendency to attribute white ethnics' economic mobility to their cultural attributes, rather than to government and the union movement, was flat-out wrong. Worse yet, it validated the War on Poverty's rejection of the kind of interventionist policies that had been indispensable to establishing the disproportionately white middle class and would have been crucial to opening pathways for low-skilled, disproportionately black workers to the stable working class and middle class.

Harrington echoed Rustin's diagnosis of both the sources of contemporary black poverty and the appropriate remedies. Like the Moynihan Report, Harrington's "The Politics of Poverty" was pessimistic about the efficacy of extant antipoverty measures. But while Moynihan's circumspection centered on the crisis in the black family, Harrington argued that "in a period of automation and cybernation" job training and tax cuts would be unable to provide sufficient economic opportunities to poor people. Drawing on the 1964 Majority Report of Senator Joseph P. Clark's Subcommittee on Employment and Manpower, Harrington observed that while output in the "non-agricultural, goods-producing sector [of] the economy" increased substantially 1957–63, "employment in this sector decreased by 300,000 jobs." The same period witnessed a rise in service and white-collar work, a pattern that dated back to 1956. Worse yet, the Department of Labor's 1965 Manpower Report noted, "even with the extraordinary stimulus of the tax cut, goods-producing industries barely held their own as a percentage of total employment." According to Harrington, then, the combination of economic stimulus and programs intended to train or even acculturate the low-skilled youth and unemployed workers—programs like Community Action preschools, Job Corps and MDTA—would do nothing to counter the decline of the manufacturing sector.[38]

Rooting black poverty in political economy, Harrington and Rustin ultimately identified a massive expansion of public-sector employment as the key to redressing disparities. Indeed, Harrington called for a Third New Deal, centered on what he referred to as a "social investment" approach. Treating the 1964

Clark subcommittee report—which laid out a plan to reduce unemployment below 3 percent by 1968 via "annual increments of $5 billion in social spending"—as a policy blueprint of sorts, Harrington argued that the GNP should be shaped not by the market but by the nation's social aims. As he succinctly stated, since the "private goods-producing sector will not create jobs for the poor . . . there must be a conscious generation of work in the public sector."[39]

If Rustin's "From Protest to Politics" provided only a glimpse of his policy prescriptions,[40] the "Freedom Budget for All" (1966) would clearly lay out his vision for combating poverty. The brainchild of Rustin, Randolph and Keyserling— Keyserling had chaired the CEA and served on President Truman's Council of Economic Advisers (1946–53)—the eighty-four-page Freedom Budget offered a detailed vision for eliminating poverty centered on redistributive programs funded by $180 billion in federal expenditures over ten years. The Freedom Budget called for full employment, a living wage, expansion of social welfare programs and massive investment in both job training and public works. Keyserling and Rustin argued that public works projects were not simply essential to combating unemployment, particularly joblessness related to automation; they also believed that such projects—which included modernizing and developing infrastructure, building schools and hospitals and revitalizing inner cities—would enhance quality of life.[41]

In an era in which Milton Friedman's vision of economic freedom is hegemonic, the aforementioned calls for redistributive approaches to poverty and unemployment have long been relegated to the political fringe. In the mid- to late 1960s, however, Killingsworth, Harrington, Randolph, Rustin and Keyserling were hardly outliers. Indeed, each of them had been well positioned in mainstream liberal political institutions; this is especially true of economists Killingsworth and Keyserling, who had chaired either economic planning or advisory committees in the Roosevelt and/or Truman administrations. Likewise, as mentioned, Secretary of Labor Wirtz and senators Clark and Humphrey had proposed redistributive policies and/or legislation that proceeded from the view that any serious effort to reduce poverty and unemployment would require public works. In this context, it should be of little surprise that the Freedom Budget had initially generated a great deal of enthusiasm and support from civil rights leaders and activists as well as many within organized labor.[42]

As the civil rights movement and the Vietnam War deepened fissures within the old New Deal Democratic coalition, support for a real assault on poverty in the form of a "Freedom Budget for All" or some other redistributive program would fade. Still, even as Nixon's 1968 election signaled the beginning of the end of New Deal liberalism, the shortcomings of the War on Poverty reflected the hegemony of a comparatively conservative approach to government stewardship of the economy—one that eschewed regulatory and redistributive policies in favor of stimulus—that, as Michael Harrington correctly argued in 1965, dated back to the Second New Deal.[43] Indeed, as historians such as Judith Russell and Judith Stein have shown, the failures of the Johnson administration's War on Poverty "on the cheap" were wed to the hubris of commercial Keynesians who were little concerned with the changing structure of the American economy.[44] Though Daniel Patrick Moynihan may have conceived *The Negro Family* as a vehicle for galvanizing support for antipoverty measures targeting African Americans, his emphasis on the distinctiveness of black poverty—his focus on black *institutional* life—rather than *economic* sources of inequality complemented the CEA's inadequate antipoverty strategy, as both divorced African American poverty from political economy.

Little more than fifty years following the publication of *The Negro Family*, Moynihan's brand of *institutional structuralism* has come to dominate discourse and policy related to poverty, a product of the "Reagan Revolution" and the ongoing rightward drift of American politics. Since the 1980s, underclass ideology—which presumed that black and brown poor people's cultural and moral deficiencies were significantly if not entirely to blame for poverty and its attendant social consequences—has served to justify the enactment of draconian drug laws, mass incarceration, cuts to public housing and social welfare programs (including the elimination of AFDC by way of the enactment of the Personal Responsibility and Work Opportunity Reconciliation Act of 1996, which then senator Moynihan ardently opposed),[45] privatization of public schools, and even the recovery efforts in Louisiana following Hurricane Katrina (August 29, 2005).[46]

In the 1960s, many of Moynihan's critics had feared that his culturalist analysis of racial inequality would not only deflect attention from the root causes of poverty but held the potential to result in either inadequate or even punitive policy measures.

Their concerns, it seems, were well founded.[47] None of this is what Moynihan had in mind, of course, but it is the logical conclusion of a perception of unemployment and low income that sidesteps the unambiguous relationship between poverty and a dearth of decent paying jobs for low-skilled workers.

4

OBAMA AND COATES: POSTRACIALISM'S AND POST-POSTRACIALISM'S YIN-YANG TWINS OF NEOLIBERAL BENIGN NEGLECT

Since the publication of "The Case for Reparations" (2014), Ta-Nehisi Coates has become one of the nation's most visible and influential African American public intellectuals. Scholars as well as liberal and even conservative pundits have hailed Coates for his courage, his passion and his insights into the history of American "race relations." Arguing that disparities in income, wealth and incarceration are generated by a trans-historical racism that has stymied blacks at nearly every turn since the colonial era, Coates rejects solutions based on broad economic redistribution. He advocates, instead, for policies targeting blacks exclusively—such as reparations—as the only feasible means of closing the material divide between African Americans and whites.

Coates's rise to prominence during President Obama's second term was, at least in part, an expression of a broadly shared disillusionment with postracialism. While pundits,

Democratic functionaries and a stratum of middle-class African American professionals celebrated the election of the nation's first black president as a transformative moment in American race relations, Obama's presidency would exert little positive influence over racial disparities. Moreover, the Tea Party and Birther movements as well as President Trump's normalization of white nationalism made clear that racial prejudice was still alive and kicking. In this context, Ta-Nehisi Coates's calls for reparations and his related embrace of racial ontology provided what many would see as a satisfying and sober alternative to postracialism.

At its core, postracialism was a reactionary fantasy. President Obama's version of it presumed that since the victories of the modern civil rights movement had swept aside the formal racial impediments to black equality, lingering inequality had less to do with extant prejudice than slow economic growth, racism's historic legacy and, crucially, the cultural deficiencies of poor African Americans themselves. Despite rhetorical nods at deindustrialization, however, President Obama—like presidents Kennedy, Johnson, Carter and Clinton before him—was little concerned with the effects of structural economic inequality. Thus, rather than demonstrating liberals' historic failure to appreciate the distinctiveness of black poverty, as Coates claims, postracialism was in step with postwar liberals' long-standing tendency to treat racial inequities as if they exist in a world apart from the economic processes that generate them. Not only does Coates's conceptualization of racism as the engine of history blind him to this fact, but his commitment to racial ontology is every bit as conservative and counterproductive as the postracialism he despises.

Barack Obama and Ta-Nehisi Coates—the very emblem of postracialism along with its most popular critic—have taken up complementary roles as black emissaries of neoliberalism. To be sure, Obama and Coates lay claim to two diametrically opposed visions of race. While Obama's postracialism traces lingering inequities, at least in part, to the cultural deficiencies of the black and brown poor themselves, Coates attributes racial disparities to an inexorable white prejudice.

Still, whether the culprit is African Americans' cultural pathologies or whites' ingrained contempt for blacks, each of these frameworks divorces what we tend to think of as racial inequality from political economy. Both Obama and Coates abstract African American poverty from the economic and social policies that have, indeed, impacted blacks disproportionately—including the decline of the union movement and the retrenchment of the public sector—even if their impetuses often have little or nothing to do with race. Rather than providing policy prescriptions that might redress the material sources of racial disparities, then, the race reductionism that informed Obama's postracialism and informs Coates's reparations agenda aids and abets a liberal politics that has been complicit in decades-long wage stagnation and the widening material gulf that separates the nation's haves from its have-nots, whatever their race.

Race and Modern Liberalism

Ta-Nehisi Coates's major works on race and American politics —"The Case for Reparations," "The Black Family in the Age of Mass Incarceration," "My President Was Black" and "The First White President"—contend that liberal social policy has failed African Americans since the New Deal because progressives have tended to view "racism not as an active, distinct evil but as a relative of white poverty and inequality."[1] According to Coates: the New Deal enshrined into law a system of entrenched inequities, via discriminatory FHA mortgage policies, that plundered black bodies and led to ghettoization; the Johnson administration ignored the urgings of assistant labor secretary Daniel Patrick Moynihan to forge a War on Poverty centered on the distinctiveness of black poverty, thereby paving the way for mass incarceration; affirmative action's promise to close the material divide between blacks and whites remains unfulfilled, thanks to its scattered focus on diversity and inclusion; and President Obama's predilection for "universal" programs—such as the Affordable Care Act (ACA), the expansion of Pell Grants and the Earned Income Tax Credit (EITC)—failed to ignite a progressive class-based coalition capable of staving off a racist, populist Trump political insurgency.

Coates's characterizations are not entirely without merit. As has been well documented by historians and social scientists, discrimination in FHA mortgage policy undercut black Americans' capacity both to accumulate wealth and to weather the withering blows of deindustrialization. The War on Poverty failed to address the root causes of black poverty, and this failure has certainly contributed to contemporary disparities in incarceration rates. Affirmative action has, indeed, proved incapable of redressing income inequality and disparities in employment. And there is little doubt that the Obama administration's tepid response to the financial crisis—along with Hillary Rodham Clinton's many flaws as a presidential candidate—helped pave the way for the faux-populist Trump presidency.

On some level, then, it is not surprising that scholars and journalists alike have lauded Coates for bringing a number of crucial issues to the attention of a broad readership. But if Coates merits recognition for introducing the ill effects of specific policies to a popular audience, his insistence that race is a force that operates independently from political economy leads him to the erroneous conclusion that modern liberalism's failures are owed to a refusal to acknowledge that racism is a distinct evil that warrants its own solutions. Indeed, as I have shown, postwar liberalism was actually characterized by a tendency to divorce race from class. Coates's fundamental claim is, therefore, incorrect. Still, in light of Coates's broad popularity and influence, it is worthwhile to explore the inadequacies of his analysis of the New Deal, the War on Poverty, affirmative action and President Obama, if only because Coates's appeal offers insights into the problems with post-postracial liberal discourse about race and inequality.

Coates's critique of the New Deal centers on two of its most documented deficiencies: the exclusion of dispropor-tionately black agricultural workers from SSA coverage and the explicit exclusion of blacks from FHA and VA mortgage policies. According to Coates, these examples highlight the limitations of universalism while demonstrating a history of white plunder of black bodies. The realities, however, are far more complicated.

As Coates correctly notes, exclusion of agricultural and domestic workers from Social Security coverage placed 65 percent of African American workers beyond the reach of the SSA's old-age retirement coverage in 1935. Drawing from the work of political scientist Ira Katznelson, Coates ultimately attributes the exclusion of agricultural and domestic workers—"jobs heavily occupied by blacks"—from the SSA to Southern Democrats' desire to infuse Jim Crow into federal policy. Though there is little doubt that Southern Democrats argued passionately against extension of Title I Social Security benefits to African Americans, the contention that racism was the principal impetus behind the SSA's exclusion of agricultural and domestic workers is difficult to defend. The most obvious problem with the claim is that it ignores the fact that the majority of sharecroppers, tenant farmers, mixed farm laborers and domestic workers in the early 1930s were white. According to the 1933 labor census, roughly 11.4 million whites were employed as farm laborers and domestic workers, compared with 3.5 million blacks. This meant that the SSA's farm and domestic exemptions excluded 27 percent of all white workers. To be sure, blacks—who were just 10 percent of the total population—were overrepresented among exempted workers, comprising 23 percent of such individuals. Whites, however, accounted for 74 percent of all workers excluded from SSA coverage.[2]

The SSA's exclusion of agricultural and domestic workers reflected a convergence of political and economic issues. Shaped partly by concerns centered on revenue collection and administration, the SSA initially extended coverage only to workers employed in commerce and industry. As a result, nearly a dozen fields—including many occupations employing few African Americans—were excluded from the SSA's purview.[3]

Opposition from employers likewise shaped the parameters of coverage. Plantation owners perceived federal welfare benefits for farm workers as a threat to their managerial prerogatives. Some proprietors already provided loyal workers in-kind benefits that were tied to their productivity. SSA coverage would necessarily undermine these incentive mechanisms.[4]

More to the point, many farm owners rejected coverage for themselves. In fact, the American Farm Bureau (AFB), the largest agricultural lobbying group of the day, not only opposed Social Security coverage for farm laborers but had successfully lobbied to exempt farm owners from coverage for nearly two decades. The AFB perceived the payroll tax as an encumbrance on business that promised few, if any, tangible rewards for proprietors.[5] While it is safe to assume that most Southern farm owners in the 1930s were racist, the fact that farm-owning proprietors generally opposed SSA coverage for farm laborers—black and white alike—as well as for themselves makes clear that their motives owed less to the "original sin of racism" than a desire to keep their labor costs down and to retain control over the operation of their farms.

Extending labor protections to sharecroppers, whatever their race, posed a threat to proprietors' managerial prerogatives. To be sure, Jim Crow buttressed the system of debt peonage that made the sharecropping system a palatable alternative to slavery for planters. But the wholesale disfranchisement of African Americans that had undercut the Populist insurgency of the last decade of the nineteenth century facilitated the expansion of a sharecropping system that, unlike slavery, exploited both black and white farm laborers.

Though FHA and VA mortgage policies are perhaps the clearest expression of what is often referred to as "institutional racism," Coates's discussion of the effects of FHA and VA mortgage policies is similarly reductionist.

In just a few decades, FHA and VA mortgages (established in 1934 and 1944, respectively) would transform a nation of renters into a nation of homeowners. In a nutshell, the FHA and VA insured mortgages against default, encouraging banks to offer homeowners long-term, low-interest loans with little money down. This in turn led to the transformation of conventional mortgages—loans not insured by the federal government— which followed federal guidelines. The federal government's transformation of the mortgage industry ultimately made homeownership a reality for millions of working-class and middle-class white Americans in the years following the New Deal. Blacks, however, were excluded from these programs— first by formal policy and then by institutional practice—until passage of the 1968 Civil Rights Act.

African Americans' exclusion from federal mortgage programs led many blacks to purchase homes on "contract" from predatory real estate entrepreneurs. Contract sellers not only retained ownership of the home until buyers had satisfied all of their obligations, but sellers generally inflated home values, charged exorbitant interest rates and levied stiff penalties—including immediate foreclosure and forfeiture of equity—for late payments. Drawing from the work of historian Beryl Satter and his own interviews with longtime residents of North Lawndale, Coates authors a vivid account of the financial damage inflicted upon the victims of contract selling as well as the destructive legacy of redlining on the West Side of Chicago. Coates offers few insights, however, into the broader dynamics shaping residential segregation. His tendency to characterize issues such as contract selling, redlining and white flight as simply further iterations of whites' "plunder" of "black bodies" belies the contingency of racist attitudes and discriminatory behavior. Indeed, by attributing housing discrimination to whites' primordial prejudice—as Coates does when he compares the motives of homeowners with slaveholders or describes white flight as a contagion[6]—Coates is free to ignore the complex political-economic underpinnings of housing discrimination.

To understand the genesis of racially stratified housing markets, there are two matters that merit particular consideration. First, Democratic and Republican administrations in the 1940s and 1950s used housing policy to nurture what would eventually be known as the Keynesian consensus. As the Great Depression was not then a distant memory, policymakers looked to spur a construction boom that might stimulate macroeconomic growth. To allay the real estate and banking industries' apprehensions about the federal government's expanding role in the nation's economy, policymakers champion the emerging housing markets not as the contrivances of federal largesse that they were, but as the release of free-market forces.[7] Second, policymakers likewise sold homeownership to America's well-unionized postwar workforce as a passport to the petit bourgeoisie. As historian Robert Self has argued, homeownership and suburbanization thus functioned to defuse labor militancy, which had reached its apex in the mid-1940s, by encouraging workers to identify with the ownership class.[8]

Though Coates sees housing discrimination as evidence of the limits of New Deal–era universalism, the postwar push for homeownership and suburbanization was actually illustrative of the shift away from the New Deal's social democratic promise. In fact, as postwar policymakers and business interests identified homeownership as a vehicle for both fostering confidence in Keynesianism and dampening working-class labor militancy, they reified housing segregation via free-market ideology. Drawing from the "market imperative" ideology pioneered by Progressive-era realtors, planners and housing economists, FHA guidelines identified nonwhites as a threat to property values. The federal government did not invent housing discrimination; however, by transforming best business practices into national policy, FHA guidelines eliminated any ambiguity about blacks' impact on local property values. Since a neighborhood's racial composition influenced home appraisals, white homeowners resisted integration via race-restrictive covenants, zoning and organized violence, or they relocated to far-flung suburbs as black neighborhoods inched ever closer, not simply because they did not like African Americans, but because they wanted to protect their investment.[9]

Understanding residential segregation in the context of housing markets places housing discrimination where it belongs, squarely in the realm of human contrivance. Contract selling was horribly exploitative. But since the evil at work here is the product of growth politics and entrepreneurialism rather than mysticism, the victims could come in many forms. Just as contract sellers fleeced black homeowners denied access to long-term mortgages, real estate entrepreneurs known as blockbusters capitalized on the vulnerabilities and fears racially tiered housing markets engendered or reinforced in white homeowners. Blockbusters purchased homes in white neighborhoods, then rented or sold the homes on contract to African Americans. Because mortgage-underwriting policy identified nonwhites as a drag on property values, blockbusters were able to rake in tidy profits by purchasing homes from panicked whites—desperate to sell before plummeting home prices wiped out all of their equity—and then gouging black renters and contract buyers.

This is not to suggest that blacks and whites were equally disadvantaged by racially stratified housing markets. They were not. The point is that Coates's narrow focus on disparities, which is a reflection on his commitment to racial ontology, leads him to misidentify the sources of the very inequities with which he is concerned. Indeed, if one considers the broad effects of both the SSA's exemptions and federal housing policy, then the disparities that Coates adduces to demonstrate racism's triumph over universalism are more accurately understood as evidence of the limits of New Dealers' commitment to regulating labor and housing markets. The SSA and FHA exemplified two different models of government stewardship of the nation's economy—the regulatory versus the compensatory state; nevertheless, both reflected New Dealers' need to accommodate capital. SSA exemptions for farm laborers helped to keep farm owners' labor costs low. The FHA's commitment to macroeconomic growth politics led it to pursue a market-oriented housing agenda that benefited banks, private developers and a variety of petty capitalists, while leaving black and sometimes even white homeowners vulnerable to predatory real estate and banking practices.

Truth be told, the exclusion of African Americans from federal mortgage policy was more devastating than Coates's focus on contract selling reveals. Denied access to affordable mortgages, urban blacks were rarely able to follow the well-paying blue-collar jobs that departed central cities for the hinterlands in the 1950s and 1960s, as neighborhoods in less densely populated suburbs were often zoned for single-family occupancy and thus excluded rentals and, by extension, most African Americans. The 1968 Civil Rights Act finally opened homeownership to blacks; however, because deindustrialization was already well underway, most poor African Americans would benefit little from access to mortgages in the absence of well-paying jobs.

Coates's commitment to treating racism and economic exploitation as discrete forces likewise contributes to his misdiagnosis of the deficiencies of the War on Poverty, leading him to an ironic, ahistorical assessment of affirmative action's limitations. Coates contends that the Johnson administration ignored Assistant Secretary of Labor Moynihan's urgings to pursue an antipoverty agenda that reflected the distinctiveness of African American poverty. As I have discussed, however, the War on Poverty actually drew heavily from Moynihan's playbook. To be sure, Moynihan became a scorned critic of the War on Poverty's expansion of social services like AFDC; nevertheless, the Johnson administration and the president's Council of Economic Advisers did indeed—much like Moynihan—attribute the high rates of black poverty in the early 1960s to the unique challenges African Americans faced in the form of racial discrimination and blacks' related soft- and hard-skills deficits. This is why programs like Job Corps and Community Action Programs emphasized provision of job training and cultural tutelage to impoverished minority youth rather than public works. The Department of Defense's Project 100,000—which lowered army entrance requirements to increase the number of black men in the military during the Vietnam era—likewise bore the influence of the only policy proposal implied by the Moynihan Report. Specifically, *The Negro Family* suggested that military service would insulate black men from the emasculating effects of racism and matriarchy, leading its author to lament the fact that African Americans' poor performance on the army IQ test reduced their share of military personnel. And while the Moynihan Report did not explicitly propose Project 100,000, secretary of defense Robert McNamara cited Moynihan as one of his inspirations.[10]

Policymakers were not inured to the hobbling effects of historic or even contemporary racism on blacks' economic prospects. The Johnson administration thus conceived of Title VII of the 1964 Civil Rights Act—the legislative basis for affirmative action—as crucial to the War on Poverty. Though Coates contends that affirmative action's focus on diversity has undercut its efficacy, he ignores the fact that diversity originated as a defensive response to the blows dealt to affirmative action by *Regents of the University of California v. Bakke* (1978) and the Reagan administration. Coates is, of course, correct to suggest that affirmative action has failed to close the material divide between blacks and whites.[11] However, the problem with Title VII is not its failure to target the specific conditions in black America but that it failed to address the principal causes of racial disparities in the 1960s—automation and deindustrialization. In other words, affirmative action reflected the Kennedy and Johnson administrations' commitment to the view that "Negro poverty is not white poverty."

In the early 1960s, many civil rights leaders were clear that antidiscrimination policies alone were incapable of closing the economic divide separating blacks and whites. Though Coates claims that A. Philip Randolph and Bayard Rustin— the organizers of the 1963 March on Washington for Jobs and Freedom—gave up their demands for race-specific remedies for black poverty when confronted with the Johnson administration's preference for class-oriented antipoverty measures, Coates's characterization actually misrepresents both sides.[12] Simply put, the black organizers of the 1963 rally identified social democratic policies as essential to redressing racial disparities in employment, income, housing and wealth, while the liberal white president opted for prescriptions that presumed the distinctiveness of black poverty and ignored the structural transformation of the economy. Indeed, even as Randolph declared his support for a fair employment practices act at the March on Washington, he stated plainly that antidiscrimination alone would do African Americans little good in the face of "profit-geared automation" that was destroying "the jobs of millions of workers black and white." Randolph and Rustin thus identified public works, full employment policies and a minimum wage hike as essential to closing the racial economic gap.[13] CORE's James Farmer, the NAACP's Roy Wilkins, and even the NUL's Whitney Young echoed Randolph and Rustin's call in 1963, as each of the above lent his support to a comprehensive antidiscrimination bill called S-1937.

In contrast to Title VII, S-1937 included job training and public works provisions. S-1937 acknowledged that racial discrimination was one of the contributors to black poverty. However, the bill's sponsors were clear that, because automation had begun to eliminate many of the low-skilled unionized jobs that had served as many whites' entry to the middle class in the 1940s and 1950s, any serious effort to redress black poverty required public works employment and targeted job training. In the wake of the Kennedy assassination and the 16th Street Baptist Church Bombing, the Johnson administration and Congress coalesced around the far less ambitious Title VII, leaving S-1937 to wither in committee.[14]

Expediency's contribution to its passage notwithstanding, Title VII reflected the Johnson administration's disregard for the implications of the structural transformation of the American economy—from manufacturing to high-tech and service—for African Americans. As I have already discussed, the administration eschewed Randolph and Rustin's calls for public works programs and instead attempted to "raise all ships" via tax-and-spend policy—commercial Keynesianism. Thus, rather than pursuing a broad redistributive antipoverty agenda that would have directly addressed the material sources of racial disparities, the Johnson administration pursued a growth-oriented antipoverty agenda that was a precursor to trickle-down.[15] This is ultimately why Randolph and Rustin proposed the "Freedom Budget for All"—a project that could hardly be considered a race-specific agenda.

In short, the Johnson administration's decision to divorce black poverty from political economy—its failure to consider the effects of automation, deindustrialization and the decline in the number of low-skilled unionized jobs on blacks—ensured that most African Americans would not benefit fully from the legislative victories of the civil rights movement. Because Coates's commitment to racial ontology shrouds the complex forces shaping African American life in a densely packed fog of black suffering and white plunder, he has difficulty making sense of the War on Poverty and affirmative action. Coates thus gives only a few passing waves at deindustrialization, despite its disproportionate impact on black Americans. In fact, Coates mentions deindustrialization fewer than half a dozen times in the more than 200 pages that comprise "The Case for Reparations" and Coates's subsequent cases for reparations—"The Black Family in the Age of Mass Incarceration" and "My President

Was Black." Needless to say, he makes many more references to the "body," "bodies" and "plunder" in these essays.[16]

Worse yet, Coates bristles at the suggestion that racial disparities should be viewed through the lens of political economy. For example, when Senator Bernie Sanders dismissed reparations as politically infeasible, arguing instead that African Americans would be better served by universal health care, a return to taxpayer-funded ("free") public higher education, a reinvigorated labor movement, revitalization of the public sector, a living wage and employment programs targeting impoverished communities, Coates not only questioned Sanders's bona fides as a progressive but he also characterized Sanders as a coward. Coates, moreover, dismissed Sanders's observation that the single-identity group focus of reparations created no basis on which to build a political coalition, claiming that Sanders's social democratic politics were no less divisive than reparations.[17] Coates, of course, has never provided compelling historical precedents for reparations. Indeed, "The Case for Reparations" offers only two examples of successful bids for such recompense, neither of which—as I will elaborate on—has any relevance to African Americans today.

Given Coates's mischaracterization of Randolph and Rustin's response to Johnson's proposed War on Poverty, it is not surprising that his critique of Sanders ignored the fact that the Vermont senator's platform not only overlapped the March on Washington's demands but also looked a lot like Randolph and Rustin's Freedom Budget. The parallels between Sanders's proposals and the Freedom Budget reflect, in part, the prescience of Randolph and Rustin's assessment of the implications of deindustrialization and the more recent retreat of the public sector for blacks.

Though unionized and blue-collar workers have become synonymous with white men in the popular imagination, since the 1970s blacks have been overrepresented among industrial and public-sector union members. Unionization has paid significant dividends to African Americans. Indeed, when compared with nonunionized black workers, black union members earn 16.4 percent higher wages, they are 17.4 percent more likely to have health insurance, and they are 18.3 percent more likely to have some form of pension. Moreover, because union contracts standardize wages, unionization virtually eliminates the black-white wage gap. Since the 1980s, however, deindustrialization[18] and corporate and public-sector retrenchment have led to a decline in the percentage of unionized black workers and, of course, the union movement in general. Whereas 36 percent of black men and 27.4 percent of black women employed in the private sector in 1983 were unionized, by 2015 the percentages had fallen to just 15 percent and 13.6 percent respectively. Black workers employed in the public sector witnessed similar declines, though today public-sector unions are far more important to black workers than their industrial counterparts.[19]

The decline of unionized manufacturing work has devastated black and brown blue-collar communities in cities such as Oakland, Chicago, Detroit, Flint, St. Louis and Coates's hometown of Baltimore. Though urban renewal helped some cities, notably Chicago, transition from manufacturing to global corporate cities, low-skilled workers benefited little from this iteration of growth politics. Indeed, the departure of unionized blue-collar jobs contributed to upticks in poverty and attendant social problems, such as crime and family dissolution in communities whose residents lacked the skills for more attractive jobs in the postindustrial economy. At the same time, the War on Crime followed by the decades-long War on Drugs would, by the early 1990s, result in the United States incarcerating more of its citizens than any other nation. Today, African Americans account for 40 percent of the nation's inmate population, followed closely by whites. But while the militarization of law enforcement and draconian sentencing for drug offenses have contributed greatly to the growth in America's prison population, here, too, bipartisan indifference to structural sources of economic inequality and the related embrace of Moynihan's contention that the poor, black or otherwise, could develop a distinctive culture that was impervious to external influence is also relevant.

The correlation between economic inequality and both violent and nonviolent crime has been well documented. However, poverty and neoliberal retrenchment have contributed to mass incarceration in other ways that are often obscured by a tendency to focus on racial disparities alone. While racism certainly plays a role in sentencing disparities, according to political scientist Marie Gottschalk, a perpetrator's class background appears to exert greater influence over incarceration rates than race. Incarceration disparities in states with comparatively poor white populations, for example, are less pronounced than in states with more affluent white populations. Likewise, racial disparities tend to be greater in states that reserve incarceration for individuals convicted of the most serious crimes, such as drug and violent offenses—the types of crimes that are more commonly committed by poor people and, by extension, blacks.[20] Since African Americans are overrepresented among the poor, budget cuts to state public defenders' offices further contribute to incarceration disparities. The decline in funding to state indigent legal services has led to a system in which 95 percent of criminal cases are settled by plea bargain.[21] Finally, mass incarceration has functioned as a dystopian accommodation to many of the problems wrought by deindustrialization and public-sector retrenchment. Large prisons not only "house" the reserve army of unemployed and—thanks to the stigma of a felony conviction—unemployable workers, but jails and penitentiaries have become major employers, particularly in rural communities. Indeed, penal Keynesianism is the lifeblood of towns like Forrest City, AR, Susanville, CA, and Marion, IL.[22]

The bottom line is that because blacks have borne a disproportionate share of the damage inflicted on working people by deindustrialization and the subsequent neoliberal economic consensus, African Americans would benefit disproportionately from Sanders's 2016 and 2020 platforms despite the absence of the reparations "brand." And while Coates claimed that Sanders's dismissal of his signature issue revealed the Vermont senator's ignorance of "the argument" for reparations, Sanders understands something that Coates refuses to acknowledge. The 64 percent of Americans who happen to be white will not tax themselves for a welfare program that they cannot, by design, benefit from irrespective of the righteousness of the cause. Righteousness was not the basis for the movements that opened opportunities to black Americans. Emancipation and even Reconstruction were produced by a convergence of interests among disparate constituencies—African Americans, abolitionists, business, small freeholders and northern laborers —united under the banner of free labor. The civil rights movement and its legislative victories—including affirmative action and the War on Poverty—were the product of a consensus created by the New Deal that presumed the appropriateness of government intervention in private affairs for the public good, the broad repudiation of scientific racism following World War II and the political vulnerabilities Jim Crow created for the United States during the Cold War. To be sure, Reconstruction, the New Deal, the War on Poverty and even the civil rights movement failed to redress all of the challenges confronting blacks. But the limitations of each of these movements reflected political constraints imposed on them, in large part, by capital.

None of this is to suggest that the elimination of economic inequality would bring about an immediate end to racism. Since the eighteenth century, Americans have viewed inequities through the lens of one formal racial ideology or another. Given racism's cultural imprint, it is safe to assume that if we were somehow able to end economic inequality next Tuesday, racial prejudice would not likely disappear on its own by next Wednesday. I am not making a case against affirmative action or other racially targeted programs. But since racial disparities in SSA coverage, access to home-ownership, unemployment and mass incarceration were or are wed to state deference to capitalist market imperatives, it

is difficult to imagine how we could eliminate racial disparities without redressing economic inequality. Indeed, the
War on Poverty and Title VII failed to eliminate economic
disparities precisely because the Johnson administration
disregarded the influence of broader economic forces on
black poverty. It is likewise difficult to imagine how one could
build a political coalition for a program that sought to insulate from capitalism's harshest conclusions a single minority
group—whose population, in contrast to investment bankers,
is overrepresented among the nation's impoverished. Should
employers have been required to pay into Social Security
for the 23 percent of farm laborers, personal servants and
domestics who happened to be black, but exempted from
payroll tax for the 74 percent of such workers who happened
to be white? Should we fund legal services at a level that
fulfills the Sixth Amendment's promise for the 40 percent of
inmates who are black, but not for the 39 percent of inmates
who are white?[23] Or should the nation pay reparations to
African Americans who were indeed fleeced by contract
sellers, but ignore those whites who sold their homes at a
loss to predatory blockbusters?

Coates's treatment of race as a force distinct from class
allows him to avoid considering such issues. And as his reflections on Obama make clear, Coates does not simply reject the
notion that race is an ascriptive category intended to denote
group members' political-economic standing, he in fact sees
race as a metaphysical force.

Obama's Metaphysical Blackness and Mythological Progressive-Universalism

"My President Was Black" echoes many of his earlier criticisms of President Obama; nevertheless, the essay also reveals Coates's affection for him. Indeed, not only do Coates's reflections on the former president hint at his admiration for Obama's intellect, his charisma and his savviness as a politician, but Coates manages to convey a feeling of kinship with the nation's first black president. What is striking about the bond that Coates feels with Obama, however, is that it is rooted in a retrograde discourse centered on cultural authenticity. Having been raised by his relatively prosperous white mother and grandparents in Hawaii, Obama had an atypical childhood characterized by lack of want and whites who loved and nurtured him. Though Coates concedes that Obama knew the sting of discrimination, he asserts, "The kinds of traumas that marked African Americans of [Obama's] generation—beatings at the hands of racist police, being herded into poor schools, grinding out a life in a tenement building—were mostly abstract for him." Instead, Obama "was gifted with a well-stamped passport and admittance to elite private schools—all of which spoke of other identities, other lives and other worlds where the color line was neither determinative nor especially relevant." Despite having the opportunity to grow "into a raceless cosmopolitan," however, Obama made what Coates describes as an admirable choice to be a part of the black community—taking his first steps down this path on the basketball court.[24]

Anyone who has actually seen President Obama should have some difficulty conceiving how he might have lived a life as a "raceless cosmopolitan." This assertion ultimately reflects Coates's conflation of both culture and class with race. He praises Obama for his decision to "download black culture" via the game of basketball and for his willingness to pay a price "for living black, for hosting Common, for brushing dirt off his shoulder during the primaries, for marrying a woman who looked like Michelle Obama."[25] For Coates, then, Obama's blackness is derived not from legal or cultural frameworks that classify people with his parentage as black; Obama's blackness is wed to his embrace of specific consumer tastes, dating choices, idiomatic expressions and, ultimately, swag. To be sure, Coates sees the aforementioned markers of racial authenticity as outgrowths of a common experience. But African Americans whose experiences deviate from what Coates sees as "the black experience" are not really black. Indeed, while Coates lauds Obama for his decision to embrace black culture, he describes the former president as less black than another African American Chicago politician, mayor Harold Washington. To be clear, Coates sees Obama as less black than Mayor Washington because Obama's experiences do not conform to Coates's view of "the black experience." And while there is little doubt that Obama's childhood paralleled that of few other black Americans, in his memoir *Between the World and Me*, Coates likewise describes the upscale African Americans in the Prince George's County of his youth—a community that is not so unusual—as essentially less black than his peers in West Baltimore.[26]

Coates's cultural nationalism leads him to view the variety of African American experiences through a lens that can pick up little more than gradations of blackness. Consequently, Coates not only misidentifies the root problems with President Obama's policy agenda but looks past the ways that Obama used the language of racial authenticity and inclusiveness to mask an agenda that could hardly be described as progressive.

Coates's approbation of Obama's decision to embrace "black culture" functions as a kind of backhanded compliment. Specifically, Coates claims that Obama's atypical experience with whites—the fact that he was raised by his nurturing white mother and grandparents—imbued him with misguided optimism about white racism. Obama, according to Coates, attributes racism to ignorance, or what Coates refers to as "white innocence." Consequently, President Obama rejected race-specific remedies for disparities such as reparations in favor of a combination of "universal programs" that African Americans would benefit from disproportionately, an aggressive nondiscrimination agenda and initiatives intended to promote personal responsibility among minority youth, such as My Brother's Keeper. Though Coates reports that Obama was not opposed to the idea of a black man's Marshall Plan, Obama argued that the absence of political will for such a program meant that the better course of action was, as Coates describes it, "to get the country to rally behind a robust liberal agenda and build on the enormous progress that's been made toward getting white Americans to accept nondiscrimination as a basic operating premise." According to Coates, however, not only does Trump's surprise win over Hillary Clinton reveal the failure of

President Obama's class-centered vision to foster interracial solidarity, but Trumpism is also illustrative of Obama's naiveté about the force of white supremacy.[27]

Though I share Coates's view that the Obama administration helped pave the way for President Trump, the claim that Obama naively pursued a progressive agenda centered on universal programs that was doomed to fail because of white racism rests on sandy ground. First, the three examples of universal programs that Obama cites and that Coates accepts as such are not what social scientists or policymakers would generally classify as "universal" programs; rather, the ACA, Pell Grants and EITC are means-tested programs. Universal programs benefit people across class lines. Means-tested programs, by contrast, target lower-income Americans. Perhaps innocent of the relevant policy nomenclature, Coates accepts the formulation and thus treats as "universal" any program that is not race-specific. By itself, this use of *universal* might appear to be nothing more than shorthand. In the context of his critique of Obama, however, Coates's failure to consider the distinction between such programs reveals an analytical blind spot. Since the intended beneficiaries of the above programs represent a fairly narrow segment of society, the ACA, Pell Grants and EITC were not likely to generate a groundswell of electoral support.

Second, Coates's contention that Trumpism is indicative of the failure of progressive class-based policies to overcome racism imputes a progressivism to Obama's domestic agenda that was not there. President Obama's push to expand Pell Grants and EITC coverage was not likely to ignite the political imagination of even the programs' beneficiaries, partly because these initiatives have been around since the 1970s. And while the ACA was the former president's signature legislative accomplishment, Obamacare is a far cry from a comprehensive national health care program like single-payer.

Rather than advancing a progressive agenda targeting the working and middle classes, Obama's economic vision—like Bill Clinton's before him—dashed the hopes of many working people for earning more than pocket change. While union members turned out for Obama in 2008 and 2012, President Obama did little to earn their support. Presidential candidate Obama courted unions with the promise of signing the Employee Free Choice Act (EFCA) and health care reform into law. EFCA would have made it easier for workers to unionize by making card check national law, brushing aside a major barrier established by Taft-Hartley (1947). Union leaders assured their members that the election of President Obama along with an enlarged Democratic majority in the Senate ensured that EFCA would become law; however, President Obama, after months of temporizing, officially pulled his support for the bill a little more than a year into his first term. Obama would, of course, follow through on his pledge for health care legislation, but rather than helping unionists, the Affordable Care Act undermined them.[28] Inspired by the right-wing Heritage Foundation and Republican governor Mitt Romney's Massachusetts Health Care Act, the ACA threatened to bankrupt union health care funds via a $63 tax imposed on each trade unionist's insurance policy. The revenue generated from the so-called Cadillac tax was conceived to finance subsidies for private for-profit insurance companies, intended to offset the expense associated with the extension of coverage to individuals with preexisting conditions. Unions' nonprofit insurance plans, however, were denied these subsidies.[29]

President Obama would also go on to champion the Trans-Pacific Partnership (TPP), which he hailed as "the most progressive trade deal in history." Though Obama claimed that the TPP would enhance national security and strengthen workers' rights and environmental regulations, the TPP would have granted more than 9,000 foreign corporations the right to circumvent regulations pertaining to labor, food and drug safety, and the environment. In other words, the TPP would have undermined democratic governance. The trade deal would also have increased the US trade deficit, resulting in the further erosion of America's manufacturing sector and an estimated loss of more than 320,000 manufacturing jobs a year.[30]

Union leaders lobbied President Obama to use his bully pulpit to press for EFCA, to amend the ACA and to reject the TPP, warning the Obama administration that its failure to look out for an important Democratic constituency might result in electoral backlash. As UNITE HERE's Donald "D" Taylor remarked in response to the administration's refusal to amend the ACA: "you can't just order people to do stuff. If their health plan gets wrecked, why would they then go campaign for the folks responsible for wrecking their health care?"[31] Obama ignored their entreaties. In fact, even as the Sanders and Trump insurgencies demonstrated bipartisan circumspection about free-trade policies—a reality that ultimately pushed centrist Democratic presidential candidate

Hillary Clinton to reject the TPP—a tone-deaf President Obama continued to stump for it.

By attributing Trump's presidential victory simply to a racist backlash against President Obama, Coates elides the implications of Obama's policies for those who rejected the third Obama term promised by Hillary Clinton. To be sure, Trump's campaign and presidency have emboldened the so-called alt-right. Former grand wizard of the Ku Klux Klan turned neo-Nazi activist David Duke's explicit affirmation of this fact the morning that neo-Nazi James Fields murdered Heather Heyer in Charlottesville, VA, only confirmed the obvious.[32] Still, the GOP has been the preferred party of organized white supremacists since Reagan, if not Nixon. So, while Trump has animated an element that has long been wed to Republicans for both ideological and opportunistic reasons, he did not escort them to the Grand Old Party.

Hillary Clinton lost the Electoral College and by extension the election because she failed to win key counties in Wisconsin, Michigan and Pennsylvania that President Obama had carried in 2008 and 2012. If one reflects on the full implications of this fact, it is hard to imagine that racism would have been the principal reason that whites who had voted for the nation's first black president would have decided, four to eight years later, to vote for its most crassly racist president in recent memory. It seems more likely that the voters Trump flipped did so because they were disillusioned with President Obama's failure to advance a policy agenda that they believed benefited them. The three counties in Pennsylvania—Erie, Northampton and Luzerne—that Trump flipped were largely blue collar.

Likewise, the dozen counties Obama carried that Clinton lost in Michigan included the Detroit suburb of Macomb and the lower-middle-class swing counties of Calhoun and Monroe. And in Wisconsin, the nearly two dozen counties Trump flipped included a few with the highest unemployment rates in the state—Sawyer, Forest and Adams.[33] Clinton's flaws as a candidate only exacerbated this problem. Her promise of a hybrid third Clinton-Obama term would have been of cold comfort to those with bitter memories of the North American Free Trade Agreement (NAFTA) as well as Obama's betrayal on EFCA and the ACA. And while Clinton reversed her position on the TPP, did anyone actually believe her—especially after she tapped Senator Tim Kaine, who supported both so-called right-to-work legislation and the TPP, as her running mate?

Given that Trump not only won a higher share of the black vote than either Romney or McCain but also performed nearly as well with black voters as George W. Bush in 2000, some African Americans may have also had bitter memories about NAFTA, EFCA and the ACA, while many of those who sat out or cast protest ballots may likewise have recalled the omnibus crime act, Rickey Ray Rector, and maybe even HOPE VI and welfare reform.

None of this is to deny that many white Trump voters—not just the Nazis—harbor noxious views about race. Treating race as if it exists in a world apart from class, however, deprives those of us who would like to live in a more egalitarian society the ability to distinguish between committed ideologues—like Nazis and Klansmen—and reflexive racists who might be won over via platforms based on common interest. Just a few months after President Trump's inauguration, Sean McElwee and Jason McDaniel argued in the *Nation* that fear of racial diversity trumped class anxiety as a motive among voters who flipped from Obama to Trump. The authors ultimately suggest that class is no longer a meaningful political category, noting that despite the fact that Democrats continue to advance progressive economic policies, non-college-educated whites trended for Trump while upscale blacks trended for Hillary Clinton.[34] As I have discussed, however, few unionists would argue that Democrats have advanced a progressive economic agenda in more than a generation. More to the point, the authors ignore the fact that "diversity" has long been synonymous with affirmative action, which conservatives have successfully—though largely disingenuously—equated with quotas and, by extension, white displacement. To whatever extent it is fair to cast fear of diversity as merely a cultural or identity issue, then, is owed largely to the fact that liberals—initially with some prodding from conservatives—have embraced a social justice discourse centered on inclusion and acceptance of group distinctiveness as an alternative to platforms centered on economic equality. This is an approach that civil rights leaders like Randolph and Rustin anticipated would not only leave most African Americans behind but would likewise foster the kind of racial animus that concerns Coates, McElwee and McDaniel.

The Underclass, Postracialism and Neoliberalism

If Coates's characterization of the progressive implications of President Obama's economic agenda misses the mark altogether, his critique of Obama's emphasis on personal responsibility is better; however, Coates's commitment to black cultural distinctiveness ensures that he is only able to graze the central problem. In recent years, Coates has been one of the more visible critics of what he calls "respectability politics." Coates is, on the whole, appropriately critical of Obama's My Brother's Keeper initiative, which he notes proceeds from the erroneous assumption that African American youth can brush aside the obstacles in their path by simply acting right. Coates is likewise appropriately critical of Obama's admonitions to poor blacks—like in his Father's Day address—to watch less TV, to stop eating Popeyes' for breakfast and to stop "blaming white people for their problems." Drawing from Obama's own words, Coates attributes the former president's naive commitment to "respectability politics" to his atypical upbringing. Obama explained to Coates that the commonplace assumption among blacks "that white people would not treat me right or give me an opportunity or judge me [other than] on the basis of merit" was less "embedded in my psyche than it is, say, with Michelle."[35] This experience, according to Coates, not only fueled Obama's commitment to universal programs, but it has imbued the former president with a misguided faith in individual solutions to societal problems.

Coates's frustration with personal responsibility ideology gives visceral voice to a long-standing problem in discourse about inequality. Still, his formulation is inadequate. Indeed, while Obama's personal experiences with the decent, professional-class whites who raised him may have informed his particular take on this issue, black politicians, scholars and commentators who have been raised by black parents—including Jesse Jackson, Cory Booker, William Julius Wilson, Roland S. Martin, Oprah Winfrey, Ben Carson and a list that could probably fill a phonebook of a Midwestern town—have espoused much the same rhetoric. The problem here, then, is not reducible to Obama's loving white mother and grandparents. In fact, if one views Obama's commitment to personal responsibility ideology in its broader political and historical context, it becomes clear that—whatever his upbringing's contribution—Obama's emphasis on individual solutions to structural problems is the product of underclass ideology.

Though the term *underclass* was coined in the 1960s, it did not gain popular use until the 1980s. Underclass ideology traced poverty to the specific cultural traits of the poor themselves. Extrapolating from anthropologist Oscar Lewis's culture of poverty thesis, proponents of underclass ideology alleged that 10–20 percent of the urban black and Latino poor were in the grip of a debilitating dysfunctional culture. Some proponents of the concept, like Charles Murray, argued that the War on Poverty's expansion of social services compounded the problem by fostering a culture of welfare dependency and a host of related antisocial behaviors—drug and alcohol dependency, promiscuity, a disregard for education and criminal activity—among poor minorities. The underclass concept meshed with Reagan's unambiguous repudiation of the idea that democratic governments should intervene in private affairs for the public good.[36] Indeed, it is no coincidence that Reagan's pro-welfare reform quip, "we waged a war on poverty [in the sixties], and poverty won," echoed a central theme of Charles Murray's

Losing Ground. While the broad coalition of Americans who embraced universal programs (entitlements) as a citizenship right preempted the neoliberal assault on Social Security and Medicare, no such breadth of support existed for the poor, disproportionately black and brown beneficiaries of the War on Poverty's and even the Nixon administration's means-tested and targeted programs. Reagan thus set his sights on dismantling jobs programs like CETA, social services like AFDC and, of course, affirmative action. Underclass ideology was pivotal to this front of the Reagan revolution, as it provided the respectable source material for racist tropes like "the welfare queen."

By the early 1990s, underclass ideology would become bipartisan consensus. In the late 1980s, black sociologist William Julius Wilson, a self-identified social democrat, helped remove the taint of racism from the underclass concept. In fact, Wilson would play a pivotal role in rehabilitating Moynihan. Wilson claimed that the backlash to the Moynihan report made liberals reluctant to acknowledge the cultural consequences of concentrated poverty, leading them to cede crucial political ground to conservatives. Wilson's *The Truly Disadvantaged* (1987) thus set out to generate support for a progressive antipoverty agenda via resurrection and update of Moynihan's culture of poverty thesis.[37] Unfortunately, the election of centrist-Democratic president Bill Clinton would reveal the inadequacy of Wilson's strategy. Bill Clinton's 1992 platform left little doubt that the Democratic party of the 1990s owed more to Reagan than Roosevelt or Johnson. Clinton—who carried a copy of *The Truly Disadvantaged* with him on the campaign

trail—echoed Wilson's concerns about crime, welfare dependency and the prevalence of female-headed households in
ghetto communities. Citing Wilson, Clinton was careful to
attribute the root causes of ghetto underclass behavior to
deindustrialization.[38] But instead of pursuing a legislative
agenda centered on bolstering the manufacturing sector or
promoting unionization, President Clinton jailed the underclass via the 1994 omnibus crime act, limited their access to
federal financial assistance via the Personal Responsibility and
Work Opportunity Reconciliation Act (1996) and razed their
homes via HOPE VI (1998). In short, if the Keynesian consensus produced an inadequate War on Poverty, the neoliberal
consensus sparked a war on the poor themselves.

Though Coates recites the oft-repeated claim that
Moynihan's advocacy of benign neglect in the Nixon years
and his 1994 remarks about poor blacks' speciation are evidence
of Moynihan's post-backlash conversion, this contention erro-
neously treats Moynihan's shift from optimist to pessimist as
if it were a transformation of his conceptual framework. *The
Negro Family* proceeded from the explicit view that sustained
poverty could generate a self-perpetuating culture that would
foil any government effort to eliminate poverty. In the 1960s,
this notion—which equated culture with race—was contested.
By the time that Hurricane Katrina made landfall in the Gulf
Coast in late August 2005, however, underclass ideology had
become hegemonic. In fact, even as underclass ideology was
at the heart of the Bush administration's and New Orleans
city officials' formal rationale for shuttering New Orleans's
public housing projects, the term *underclass* was scarcely used,

as poor black and brown people had now become synonymous with dysfunction.

By 2008, "serious" black Democratic and Republican politicians—biracial or not—reflexively traded in underclass narratives. Barack Obama, however, did so with a finesse and polish that political commentators and fellow Democrats alike believed augured a transformative, postracial era of American politics. Indeed, Obama's election promised to harmonize political discourse on racial and economic inequality, as his presidential campaign and presidency would further legitimate underclass ideology's project of racializing economic inequality via attribution of poverty to the dysfunctional culture of the minority poor themselves rather than political economy. Obama's contribution would take two forms. First, like a long line of Democrats before him, Obama would emphasize— albeit with quick nods to institutional racism and a soupçon of compassion—the impact of ghetto residents' dysfunctional behavior on contemporary disparities as a pretext for stressing individual solutions to structural problems.

In his breakthrough 2004 DNC keynote, for example, Obama expressed compassion for implicitly white blue-collar workers devastated by the offshoring of unionized jobs; he sympathized with hardworking Americans who could not afford necessary prescription drugs; and he empathized with suburban voters who objected to their taxes going to welfare or wasteful military projects. By contrast, Obama's reflections on implicitly black "inner-city" residents stressed the need for African Americans to extricate *themselves* from dysfunction: "Go into any inner-city neighborhood, and folks will tell you that government alone can't teach kids to learn." Obama then continued, "They know parents have to parent, that children can't achieve unless we raise their expectations and turn off the television sets and eradicate the slander that says a black youth with a book is acting white."[39]

Though Obama's chastisement of "inner-city" residents could be read as a counter to Reagan's welfare queen, "A More Perfect Union," Obama's much-lauded March 2008 race speech, made clear that his admonitions were capitulations to the racist underclass trope. Delivered on the heels of the Reverend Wright controversy, Obama's race speech was intended to both sever his association with the "militant" minister and position Obama as a healer of racial wounds. To this end, Obama would paint a vivid landscape of transgenerational black social pathologies. Specifically, Obama would attribute Wright's indefensible sermon—damning America for its history of racism in conspiratorial terms—to the psychic scars of wounds inflicted in the Jim Crow era. Obama claimed that many black men and women of Wright's generation were trapped in a loop of traumas long since passed. While Jim Crow had been defeated during the 1960s, its traumatic legacy could be observed in America's inner cities today. After making fleeting references to the long-term consequences of discriminatory mortgage policy and the dearth of employment opportunities for young black men, Obama would turn his attention to contemporary black dysfunctionality. Rather than stressing the material impact of poverty and unemployment on family dissolution, for example, Obama insinuated that the *shame* felt by those black men who were inadequate providers was a major contributor to the erosion

of the African American family. From there, Obama went on
to imply his support for Clinton's 1996 welfare reform act,
asserting "that welfare policies had for many years" undermined
African American family formation. Obama continued with an
acknowledgment that declining support for social services had
contributed to the challenges confronting urban black communities. But rather than critiquing the neoliberal consensus that
was at the heart of the decades-long retreat of the public sector,
Obama asserted a link between the atrophy of social services
and a self-perpetuating "cycle of violence, blight and neglect
that continues to haunt us."[40]

Obama's 2008 Father's Day remarks before the Apostolic
Church of God in Chicago read from much the same playbook.
After reciting the standard litany of inner-city social problems
—high rates of teen pregnancy, female-headed households,
poverty and unemployment, crime, school dropouts and incarceration—Obama once again delivered a short paragraph
acknowledging that gun control along with increased funding
for education, social services, law enforcement and job training
programs might alleviate some of these problems. Obama
then dedicated the next twenty-two paragraphs to lecturing
African American fathers about the importance of personal
responsibility, arguing that the failure of too many black men to
instill values of excellence, empathy, hope and self-reliance in
their children was a key contributor to ghetto social malaise.[41]

Obama's disposition to scold inner-city minorities did not
preclude the helping hand of government. However, when
combined with his Jedi-mind-trick-like assertion—like in his
2004 DNC address—that inner-city residents did not expect

government to solve *all* of their problems, Obama's embrace
of underclass ideology signaled to Democrats and even conservatives that he, like Bill Clinton before him, had little interest
in redressing the material roots of inequality.

The second contribution Obama's postracial presidency
made to the ongoing project to divorce racial inequality from
class inequality came in the form of his race and his biography.
While Bill and Hillary Clinton's whiteness left them, or any
other non-black president or presidential candidate, vulnerable
to pushback from a reliable Democratic constituency, Obama's
actual blackness and his related "performance of blackness"
insulated his accounts of African American social pathology
and related calls for personal responsibility from the charge
of racism. To be clear, I am not questioning Obama's racial
"authenticity." To the contrary, since race is an ascriptive category, Obama is unquestionably black, in my view, irrespective
of his personal predilections or behavior. But in order for
Obama to be an effective postracial champion of personal
responsibility, his biography had to read like the underclass
version of a Horatio Alger novel. This would require that
Obama project what "blackness" had come to mean in the
popular conscience. In other words, America had to accept
Obama as a man who *could have* easily become "a statistic," a
stereotype, but managed to extricate himself from the tangle
of pathologies that ensnared so many of his brothers and
sisters. We had to see Obama as yet another black man who had
struggled with frustration and anger, who had experimented
with drugs and who had been unsure of the value of formal
education because he had been abandoned by his irresponsible

black father and raised by his (white) single mother and (white) grandparents. We had to believe that Obama had the strength of character to overcome the odds, to go on to earn degrees from two Ivy League universities and ultimately to become the first black US president.

Obama did not lie about his background. However, he frequently pitched his biography at a level of abstraction that blurred the line between his truth and the mythical "Cousin Pookie." Indeed, the details of Obama's biography reveal the importance of class privilege to his success. Obama's parents did not meet in high school or even "at the club"; they met in college. Obama's father did abandon him and his mother; however, it was not because he was ashamed of his meager wages or because he had to do a bid in a state or federal penitentiary, but he left his son and wife to attend graduate school at Harvard. Obama's mother surely experienced financial struggles, but she would go on to earn advanced degrees after remarrying a well-educated and prosperous Indonesian businessman. Obama's grandparents did help raise him, but they were solidly middle class or better. Obama may have had some doubts about the value of formal education as a young man, but he struggled with them in one of Hawaii's most prestigious prep schools. And sure, Obama smoked weed while he was in prep school and college, but good luck finding a white graduate of an expensive liberal arts college or Ivy League university who did not experiment with drugs or alcohol as an undergraduate.

The particulars of Obama's compelling biography should have undercut the sway of his underclass-inflected Horatio

Alger success story. The abstract biographical sketch was, however, crucial to his star power, as it not only made Obama the multicultural exemplar of the classic American success story, but it conferred to him the authority to admonish poor African Americans for their alleged cultural deficiencies. Indeed, the enthusiasm that Democrats and pundits like Senator John Kerry, Glenn Greenwald, Matt Bai and conservative David Brooks expressed for him during the 2008 presidential campaign made clear that Obama's willingness to use his alleged moral authority to chastise black voters was a major source of the appeal of his postracial presidency.[42]

Since Obama's class privilege could have left him open to questions about his racial authenticity with far too many African Americans—even if both of his parents had been black—his biographical sketch offered some cover with black voters.[43] There was, of course, no way to finesse the fact that Obama was a biracial man who grew up in Hawaii, which meant the sketch alone could not suffice. Obama's efforts to position himself as a postracial president thus required that he perform blackness. In other words, Obama draped himself in tropes of "the black experience." To have the kind of political career Obama wanted, he needed to join Trinity United Church of Christ and, in Coates's words, he needed to marry a black woman who looked like Michelle. This is also why it was savvy of Obama to hang out with Common, Jay-Z and Beyoncé (three famous "authentically black" rich people) and to "brush dirt off his shoulder" while the cameras were rolling. Had Obama failed to appreciate the fact that, at this point, far too many Americans conflate culture with race, black voters might have noticed—long before George Zimmerman's acquittal in the Trayvon Martin murder trial—that the nation's first black president had campaigned on a pledge to accommodate them to a Bill Clinton–esque neoliberal agenda that would do little to redress the kind of material issues, such as poverty and unemployment, that impacted African Americans disproportionately.

Indeed, the combination of Obama's use of the underclass metaphor and his actual and "performed" blackness gave him a comparatively free hand with which to craft an agenda intended to right a listing American economy, absent the kinds of redistributive policies—like revitalization of the public sector, support for unionization, opposition to free trade, mortgage relief and so on—that would have benefited blacks disproportionately precisely because they are overrepresented among neoliberalism's victims. To be sure, people who identify as "African American activists"—as opposed to, say, those who might identify as black union organizers—are far more likely to make demands for issues such as mortgage relief in terms that center on racial grievance rather than economic inequality. This is one of the reasons that liberals and even many conservatives found the prospect of an Obama presidency appealing.

When President Obama took office in January 2009, the nation's economy was a wreck. If president George W. Bush's efforts to stimulate economic growth via policies designed to swell the ranks of homeowners created a housing bubble, President Clinton's repeal of Glass-Steagall ensured that when Bush's bubble burst its effects would ripple through the entire economy. Many Americans had hoped that the high-minded

Obama would respond to the crisis by drawing from the New Dealers' playbook. Unfortunately, he did not. While President Obama did follow through on measures intended to stabilize the US economy—the banking and auto-industry bailouts and the stimulus package surely stemmed the bleeding and saved many jobs—they did not address the structural issues that were the root causes of decades of depressed wages. In fact, in contrast to the Roosevelt administration, the Obama administration eschewed labor and housing market reforms that might have shored up the nation's precarious working and middle classes while opening pathways to the middle class for the working poor and unemployed. Unions, as I have discussed, did not receive the support President Obama had promised. Though Obama had earmarked $100 billion of the Troubled Asset Relief Program (TARP) for mortgage relief, by the end of his second term only $21 billion of these funds had been released. Consequently, fewer than 1 million of the 4 million mortgage modifications that Obama had promised had been completed by President Trump's election. Even the stimulus package was inadequate for the crisis at hand. In fact, economist Paul Krugman had warned as early as January 2009 that the $787 billion stimulus provided by the American Recovery and Reinvestment Act (ARRA) would surely help, but that in taking such a conservative approach—not only was the package too small, according to Krugman, but 40 percent of the stimulus took the form of tax cuts—Obama would fail to stimulate meaningful economic growth and thus squander a political opportunity. Specifically, Krugman feared that an anemic recovery generated by a stimulus that was only large enough to arrest the economic slide but too small to reduce unemployment and boost consumer purchasing power would be cast by the right wing as yet another example of the failure of big government.[44]

Just shy of a month into President Obama's first term, CNBC's Rick Santelli's call for a Tea Party movement—delivered on the floor of the Chicago Stock Exchange—would mark the realization of Krugman's fears. Though the Tea Party's roots stretched back to the 1990s, the Koch brothers–funded "movement" capitalized on the economic and racial anxieties of conservative voters. The Tea Party's anti-tax, small government agenda may not have been formally racist; however, well before anyone imagined that Americans were willing to elect a black president, conservatives had succeeded in equating big government, high taxes, welfare and Democrats with an approach to governance that benefited irresponsible African Americans and poor people at the expense of the implicitly white, sober middle class. Santelli's condemnation of President Obama's mortgage relief program as a boon to profligate losers financed at the expense of responsible, hardworking Americans thus only hinted at a conservative *racial* backlash. Tea Party darling Michele Bachmann, however, had no compunction about casting the financial meltdown in explicitly racial terms.[45]

The combination of the Tea Party movement's racist subtext, the Birther movement's racist text, George Zimmerman's shocking acquittal and a seemingly interminable stream of video footage of police officers murdering or assaulting unarmed, disproportionately black people literally broadcast the absurdity of postracialism. Moreover, since Obama's presidency would produce few material benefits for most blacks, the limitations of his symbolic racial victory became clearer even to African Americans who had initially accepted him as role-model-in-chief. Indeed, both because poverty rates were on an upward swing when Obama took office and because his administration did little to redress the structural sources of economic inequality, the percentage of African Americans living in poverty was actually higher when Obama left office than when he assumed it. The cumulative effects of the racially inflected political backlash to America's first black president, along with perpetual disparities in the criminal justice system and in the nation's poverty and unemployment rates, led many African Americans and even some whites to conclude that Obama's conciliatory postracialism not only was naive but also ignored entrenched structural racism.

Reparations, Racial Ontology and Neoliberal Benign Neglect

Ta-Nehisi Coates's influence among liberals is among the clearest expressions of the breadth of disillusionment many Americans felt in the post-postracial era. While Coates's career as a journalist and essayist dates back to the late 1990s, the 2014 publication of "The Case for Reparations" catapulted him to stardom. His reparations essay and his subsequent major works stand in sharp contrast to the postracial promise of the Obama presidency. Whereas postracialism proceeded from the view that the victories of the civil rights movement had swept aside the major barriers to racial equality for those willing to take advantage of the opportunities before them, Coates's essays presume that racism is embedded in the very structure of American society. Slavery, Jim Crow, FHA mortgage discrimination, disparities in wealth and employment and mass incarceration are all, in Coates's view, evidence of a systemic racism that has excluded blacks from the promise of American liberty since the nation's founding.

As I have discussed, Coates's historical and political analyses are inadequate. His contention that racism has prevented universal programs from distributing rewards equitably to blacks and whites obscures the economic imperatives undergirding racial discrimination in housing and labor markets. Coates's critiques of the War on Poverty and President Obama likewise fail to consider the distinction between growth politics and redistributive politics. To be sure, Coates has authored a number of impassioned pleas for reparations centered on visceral accounts of black suffering from slavery through the start of the Trump administration. The particular mechanisms that drive the forms of disadvantage that blacks confront in one era as compared with another, however, are of little concern to him.

What is perhaps most striking about Coates's "The Case for Reparations" is that it is not really a case for reparations at all. As I've alluded to, Coates cites only two historical precedents for reparations. The first example is the case of former slave Belinda Royall who, in 1783, successfully petitioned the Massachusetts legislature for financial support for herself and her infirm daughter. As Coates makes clear, the state legislature ultimately decreed that Royall would be paid a monthly pension from the estate of Isaac Royall, Belinda's loyalist former master. The second example Coates presents is Germany's restitution to Holocaust survivors and Israel. Since 1953, Germany has paid about $90 billion in reparations to victims of the Holocaust and Israel. Coates observes that Germany's restitution payments to Israel helped shore up the fledgling Jewish state by financing vital infrastructure projects. Although Coates holds up the Royall case and Holocaust restitution as evidence of reparations' viability, he eschews exploration of the politics undergirding these examples.

Coates's discussion of the Royall case, for example, does not mention that her entreaty was steeped in the language of republican virtue and patriarchal obligation, as the former slave detailed her vulnerability as an aged woman who, having only recently been manumitted, possessed neither husband nor property. Likewise, despite the fact that Belinda Royall's successful petition for recompense was granted the very same year that the Massachusetts high court declared slavery unconstitutional (1783), Coates gives no consideration to the fact that the Royall judgment was illustrative of a wave of antislavery sentiment—triggered by the democratic impulses that informed America's war for independence—that swept across New England and the mid-Atlantic states during and immediately following the revolution. And while Coates mentions that Royall's former master had been a loyalist, he does not reflect on how this might have influenced the Royall act. Indeed, a judgement for Belinda Royall was as much an indictment of a traitor to the revolution as it was a repudiation of slavery.

Likewise, Coates lauds the Federal Republic of Germany's

(FRG) decision to make restitution to both victims of Nazi genocide and the newly formed Jewish state but curiously offers no material explanation for West Germany's motives. Prior to the 1952 Luxembourg Agreement, conquered nations had paid restitution to their wartime adversaries—that is, nation-states. The FRG's decision to make restitution to Israel—which was founded three years *after* the Third Reich's defeat—and to individual victims of Nazi atrocities, then, was a bold departure from precedent. Even if we assume Coates's contention that reparations helped "launch Germany's reckoning with itself" is accurate, the FRG agreed to make restitution because it was under political pressure to distance itself from Nazi atrocities. Not only had Nazi Germany attempted to exterminate racial groups and other populations that the regime had deemed threatening or unfit, but the Third Reich had engaged in an expansionist war against nations that were to become West Germany's Cold War allies. In 1949, the year the FRG was established, many leaders in Europe and the United States were circumspect about the reemergence of a German state in the West. Western allies thus compelled the FRG to make restitution to Holocaust victims as a condition for both its full sovereignty and the end of West Germany's occupation. So, when the Israeli government broached the topic of Holocaust restitution, the FRG was in a particularly vulnerable position. West Germany made restitution to Jewish victims of the Holocaust and Israel, then, not simply because it was the "right thing to do," but because reparations constituted partial down payment on the fledgling FRG's independence.[46]

The details of these two cases make clear that they fail as

precedents for African American reparations. Not only is there no contemporary equivalent to the political antislavery movement that had informed the Royall act, but—in contrast to Belinda Royall—the more than 40 million blacks in the United States cannot expect restitution from traitors to the nation's independence. Likewise, in contrast to postwar Germany, the US is the world's dominant ideological, financial and military power. The nations with which we have warred over the past few decades are, thus, in no position to pressure the US—indirectly or directly—to make restitution to African Americans. Because Coates's ontological commitment to race can only permit a politics of moral pleading, the specific material and ideological issues that inform political decisions are inconsequential. The only details that matter to him are the grievance and the justness of the cause.[47] Coates's narrow focus on the righteousness of these cases ultimately allows him to insinuate parallels between them and the case for African American reparations in the absence of a material basis for comparison. And since reparations presumes that whites' pathological commitment to white-skin privilege precludes political alliances—short lived or otherwise—based on mutual interest, Coates's case for recompense *has to* center on special pleading.

But pleading is not politics and Coates's case for reparations is not a blueprint for a feasible political movement. If, as Coates argues, the white working and middle classes are so racist that they elected Donald Trump to erase the allegedly progressive economic agenda implemented by the nation's first (neoliberal) black president, then why would they support reparations—a program from which they could never benefit? While Coates may believe that moral suasion is the engine of political change, the historical record makes clear that coalitions built on mutual interest, rather than the kind of altruistic noblesse oblige reparations would require, have been essential to blacks' material advancement. Reparations' appeal, however, is not rooted in its feasibility. This is why the absence of historical precedent for Coates's formal case for reparations is ultimately beside the point. Whatever Coates's intent, the appeal of his work is owed, in large part, to reparations' political *infeasibility*. Indeed, "The Case for Reparations" and all of Coates's subsequent related essays are less calls to arms to end racial disparities than a case for a national conversation about race—albeit under a different name.

At its most ambitious, Coates's formal case for reparations is merely a call for moving representative John Conyers's HR 40 out of committee—where, recent congressional hearings notwithstanding, it has languished, in one form or another, since 1989—to debate on the floor of the House of Representatives. Coates's reflections on HR 40 make clear that he is willing to settle for far less than material redress. Conyers's bill does not outline a schedule for restitution; it simply calls for exploring the feasibility of reparations. Still, Coates contends that moving the bill out of committee alone will pay dividends for both blacks and whites. Describing reparations as "the full acceptance of our collective biography—the price we must pay to see ourselves squarely," Coates implies that material compensation may not be a necessary fix for black suffering. "Perhaps after a serious discussion and debate—the kind that HR 40 proposes," he says, "we may find that the country can never fully repay African Americans. But we stand to discover much about ourselves in such a discussion." Insinuating that the exercise alone has the potential to check racism's eternal sway, Coates asserts that "the recovering alcoholic may well have to live with his illness the rest of his life. But at least he is not living a drunken lie."[48]

Coates's penchant for substituting metaphor for analysis is more than mere rhetorical flourish. His reliance on moralistic abstractions not only allows him to skirt the political challenges that would confront a movement centered on material compensation for African Americans alone but also accommodates bipartisan indifference to the damaging effects of neoliberal economic and social welfare policies on disproportionately black and brown working people. Leaving little doubt that his case for reparations owes more to Dr. Phil or perhaps even the Rite of Exorcism than the Freedom Budget, Coates concludes his discussion of Conyers's HR 40 by declaring: "What is needed is an airing of family secrets, a settling with old ghosts. What is needed is a healing of the American psyche and the banishment of white guilt."

Whereas President Obama's soaring postracialism licensed the continuation of liberal indifference to the plight of economically marginal people via underclass metaphors, Coates's post-postracial commitment to racial ontology signs off on white liberal hand-wringing and public displays of guilt as alternatives to practicable solutions to disparities. To be sure, this is not Coates's formal intent, even if the words on the page imply that Coates might find a racial Festivus to be an acceptable alternative to material compensation. But because reparations is a political dead end, Coates is offering white liberals—and even a stratum of conservatives—who are either self-consciously or reflexively committed to neoliberal orthodoxies absolution via public testimony to their privilege and their so-called racial sins.

Some will surely take exception to the claim that Coates adduces only two historical precedents for reparations. Indeed, in addition to the restitution paid to Belinda Royall and Germany's reparations to Jewish victims of the Holocaust and Israel, Coates does reference instances in which individual slaveholders, struck by pangs of conscience, manumitted their slaves as well as more recent housing discrimination settlements made by the Bank of America (2011) and Wells Fargo (2012) in the wake of the subprime mortgage crisis. Rather than constituting examples of successful bids for reparations, however, these cases are best understood as individual charitable acts and torts respectively. Coates's moralistic account—wed, as it is, to the reparations "brand"—creates some ambiguity about the distinctions between charity and torts, on the one hand, and state-centered recompense (what reparations would have to be), on the other. Nevertheless, Coates's ambivalence about what reparations would actually look like and, of course, the related implication that either enforcement of extant antidiscrimination laws or charity might constitute acceptable recompense does poor and working-class African Americans a major disservice. Specifically, Coates's fuzziness about the substance and scope of appropriate restitution for America's "racial sins" opens the door to simply rebranding as "reparations" remedies—as several 2020 Democratic presidential hopefuls have already done—that have long failed to meet the material needs of the masses of poor and working-class black and brown people.

The combination of Coates's apparent sincerity and his racial militancy help to obscure reparations' conservatism. Its militant trappings notwithstanding, reparations—a project that presumes the realness of race (the permanency of racism) and the sanctity of private property—is a fundamentally reactionary political program. Coates is no less fond of tales of black pathology than President Obama, even if Coates chooses to admonish whites instead of poor blacks. Indeed, Coates's accounts of the material "plunder" of black bodies are often wed to the psychological trauma inflicted upon African Americans—from the fear-fueled beatings he received at the hands of his father to the hypermasculine bravado that he inaccurately describes as a uniquely black male street code.[49] Commentators ranging from Michelle Alexander to David Brooks have thus frequently remarked on the anger and frustration that permeates Coates's prose, as Coates both voices and personifies black alienation. It should go without saying that many black Americans, myself among them, are justifiably frustrated about disparities, the rise of a much emboldened far right, and liberals' failure to deliver on promises to ameliorate inequality. But by embracing a framework that presumes that African Americans are frustrated by an eternal white racism, abstracted from political economy, Coates paints a picture of perpetual black alienation that reinforces—his good intentions notwithstanding—the underclass framework that has contributed to liberals' and conservatives' failure to redress structural sources of inequality.[50]

Moreover, Coates's disposition to dismiss those who identify social democratic policies as the most feasible and effective vehicle through which to bolster African Americans' material standing reveals his own ironic commitment to bourgeois politics. While he offers his white, white-collar, cosmopolitan readers absolution, Coates legitimates contempt for the white working class. As I have discussed, Coates's contention that Trump's strong showing with working-class whites in the 2016 presidential election revealed the depth of their commitment to white-skin privilege and the futility of interracial class politics imputes an economic progressivism to President Obama and the Clintons that was not there. But by attributing Hillary Clinton's loss, at least in part, to a pathologically racist white working class that regularly votes against its own economic interests, Coates legitimates a neoliberal agenda—embraced by the Clintons, Obama and the DNC—that has come to treat identity politics as the realpolitik alternative to a progressive, truly universal, economic program promising tangible rewards for working people. Indeed, during the 2016 presidential primary, both Coates and the Clinton campaign chastened Senator Sanders and his supporters for allegedly deflecting attention from structural racism.

If one reflects on Hillary Clinton's attachments to underclass-fueled rationales for the omnibus crime act, Clinton and her surrogates' criticisms of Sanders and his supporters were transparently disingenuous. The motives behind Coates's criticisms, by contrast, seem to stem, at least partly, from his belief that a politics centered on workers' rights is necessarily antagonistic to policies like affirmative action. As I discussed in Chapter l and elsewhere, however, the groundwork for affirmative action, whatever its limitations, was laid by the New Deal. The 1935 National Labor Relations Act established a precedent for government intervention into the employer-employee relationship for the public good. Just as the right to collective bargaining constituted an exception to "liberty of contract," so, too, does antidiscrimination legislation.[51]

The parameters and function of even targeted programs are necessarily shaped by their broader political and ideological context. Coates's commitment to racial ontology, however, precludes any serious attempt to either ground racism in the material world or to historicize liberal policy prescriptions beyond their failure to redress disparities. But if the endgame is to address the economic disadvantages that blacks face and, by extension, the attendant social problems that afflict lower-income black and brown communities disproportionately, it is difficult to see how the neoliberal consensus — which is antagonistic to the notion of government intervention for the public good—could engender targeted initiatives that benefit poor and working-class blacks rather than elites. Indeed, it is no coincidence that affirmative action's focus shifted from material redress to diversity at the dawn of American neoliberalism. It is likewise no accident that in an era in which neoliberalism has become hegemonic, social justice has come to merge with entrepreneurialism—producing a "progressive" politics that not only casts charter schools, NGOs and sundry internet startups as alternatives to state action but lionizes black/brown businesspeople (including the occasional rap and R&B mogul) as the new generation of civil rights leaders.

Reparations' repudiation of postracialism's absurd claim that the principal obstacles confronting blacks in the twenty-first century are poor blacks' social pathology and middle-class blacks' anachronistic cynicism is not without value. When articulated by the nation's first "authentically" black president, postracialism legitimated the Democratic commitment to neoliberal economic and social welfare policies that promised poor blacks few, if any, material rewards and middle-class blacks a seat at a shrinking table. Coates's instincts about the limitations of personal responsibility ideology, then, are basically correct. Unfortunately, the benefits derived from Coates's critique of postracialism's basic tenets are more than offset by the problems engendered by his commitment to ontological racism. Specifically, not only does Coates's insistence that race operates independently of economic exploitation obscure the cause of these inequities, but his mystification of race permits no tangible solutions. I will take a moment to channel the spirit of Phaedra Parks and bluntly state that everybody knows that reparations, in the form of a redistributive agenda that would only benefit African Americans, ain't gonna happen—certainly Coates's white readers know this. But consider what that means. Coates identifies reparations as the only fix for the racial inequities that he traces to an ineradicable racism. Since reparations is not a feasible politics, Coates's fatalism about racism—his good intentions notwithstanding—licenses perpetual inequality. Simply put, if white racists will always be with us, as Coates suggests, then poor blacks will always be with us, too.

Postwar liberal orthodoxies have failed to redress racial

disparities. The culprit, however, is not the sway of a meta-physical racism, but rather the roots of contemporary dispar-ities can be traced to far more comprehensible forces such as: the tensions within the New Deal between the regulatory and compensatory state models and the related mid-century tensions between industrial and commercial Keynesians; the contrasting influences of the New Deal and the Cold War on the parameters of liberal discourse about race and inequal-ity; and neoliberalism's rise from the ashes of the Keynesian consensus. In other words, the problem is not, as Coates insists, that liberals have long attempted to redress black poverty by reducing racism to class exploitation, resulting in universal policies that focus on economic sources of inequality as an alternative to addressing racism. Indeed, since the 1960s, liberal policymakers have generally ignored the impact on African Americans of issues such as deindustrialization, the decline of the union movement and retreat of the public sector. The Keynesian consensus still allowed liberals of the 1960s and 1970s to pursue antipoverty policies centered on the expan-sion of social services and even state-centered regulation of employer-employee relations via affirmative action; however, the neoliberal consensus ensured that centrist-Democratic presidents Bill Clinton and Barack Obama would pursue agendas that chipped away at the public-good framework that established the rights and protections that have benefited disproportionately black, poor and working-class Americans at the very same time they either championed or personified diversity.

In this context, Coates's insistence that so-called racial issues exist in a world apart from economic issues is not a critique of postwar liberalism but is, at best, a call for continuing along the same path that has failed most black Americans since the Johnson administration. At worst, it is a call for no more than ritualized acknowledgment of white privilege and black suffering.

Racial ideology does indeed inform how we perceive people and their place in the pecking order, as is its purpose. Racism thus influences inequities. It does so, however, within a larger political-economic framework. Efforts to redress racial disparities that do not consider the work that race does in American labor and housing markets will be doomed to fail, just as they have since the War on Poverty. So, while it is unlikely that Coates set out to be neoliberalism's most visible black emissary of the post-postracial era, his insistence that we must treat race as a force that exists independently of capitalism has, ironically, earned him this accolade.

CONCLUSION: RACE REDUCTIONISM AND THE PATH TO PRECARITY FOR ALL BUT A DIVERSE FEW

To say that Donald Trump's surprise win over Hillary Clinton has undermined the possibilities for better politics would be an understatement. It's not that a Clinton presidency would have ushered in a wave of progressive policies—it would not. But Trump's faux-populist pitch to the "little guy" notwithstanding, the "stand-up philosopher" president's legislative agenda as well as his cabinet and Supreme Court appointments are about as reactionary as they come.

Indeed, Trump's first attorney general, Jeff Sessions, was unabashedly antagonistic to laws protecting the rights of people of color, women and LGBTQ individuals. Trump's secretaries of the Environmental Protection Agency (EPA), the Department of Education (ED), Department of Labor (DOL) and the Department of Housing and Urban Development (HUD) are either stridently or reflexively antagonistic to the very agencies that they now head. The first of at least two justices that President Trump and the Republican Senate have appointed to the United States Supreme Court, Neil Gorsuch, predictably cast the deciding vote in *Janus v. AFSCME*—a major blow to public-sector unions. And the hits to labor, civil rights, reproductive rights, environmental protection, education, housing and many other areas will surely just keep on coming as long as Trump is president.

Still, the legislative and judicial implications of the Trump presidency for workers' rights, civil rights and public-sector retrenchment are not much different from what we could have expected from a Jeb Bush or a Ted Cruz presidency.[1]

Trump has, however, had a *distinctly* negative impact on the scope of progressive political discourse. If the Sanders insurgency galvanized centrist-Democrats to coalesce around fundamentally conservative race reductionist frameworks, Donald Trump's victory over Secretary Clinton has encouraged mainstream Democrats to double down. Indeed, corporate Democrats and even many liberal-left identitarians have cast Trump's victory as evidence of the supremacy of white-identity politics and the irrelevance of economic class as a basis for political mobilization.

While those insisting that ontological race/racism is the engine of human history generally also reject the value of interracial political coalitions centered on the shared material concerns of poor and working-class people (groups in which blacks are overrepresented), they frequently use the language of disparities and diversity to advance their own reactionary class agenda. Indeed, race reductionists are not simply circumspect about the kind of redistributive politics that would benefit black and brown people disproportionately (though not uniquely)—they are dismissive of, if not outright antagonistic, to such policies.

As I have discussed, both President Obama's postracial presidency and Ta-Nehisi Coates's post-postracial reparations politics have complemented neoliberalism's market-friendly, anti-welfare state politics while offering poor and working-class African Americans cathartic symbolic or rhetorical wins as alternatives to substantive improvements in their material lives. Given that 2020 Democratic presidential hopefuls Cory Booker, Pete Buttigieg, Julian Castro, Kamala Harris, Elizabeth Warren and Marianne Williamson have each expressed interest in reparations as part of a larger conversation on the racial wealth gap, some will blanch at this statement. But the devil is in the details. Indeed, with the exception of long-shot candidate Marianne Williamson, none of the above has proposed anything reasonably understood as reparations. Instead, the competitive candidates have each laid out a mix of means-tested and targeted programs, *branded* as reparations, as alternatives to the kind of universal redistributive programs from which blacks would disproportionately benefit.

Progressive Elizabeth Warren's proposals for closing the racial wealth gap offer perhaps the clearest window onto reparations' rightward pull on contemporary political discourse. Senator Warren has not only called for a $7 billion intraracial trickle-down program intended to infuse wealth into "the black community" by growing the ranks of black/brown entrepreneurs, but her narrow focus on the racial wealth gap has led her to reject universal student loan forgiveness—claiming that elimination of *all* student loan debt would exacerbate the racial wealth gap—in favor of her means-tested proposal.[2] If one considers the abysmal first-year failure rate among new businesses and small business owners' notorious antagonism to living-wage policies, it's not clear that growing the ranks of black/brown entrepreneurs would translate into good jobs for a meaningful number of black/brown workers. Likewise, since African Americans are much more likely than whites to finance their educations with federal loans, blacks would actually benefit disproportionately from universal debt forgiveness.[3]

So, while there is no denying the fact that the Trump presidency has been a boon to the reparations *brand*, even if reparations (a cash transfer from whites to African Americans) still ain't gonna happen, reparations' resonance in this moment is but one of many expressions of liberals' and even left-identitarians' commitment to racialist understandings of the world that not only look past the material and political implications of the American liberal/left's long retreat from class politics but also license disregard and, in some cases, outright contempt for working-class and poor people irrespective of race.

If there is a silver lining to be found in this bleak reality, it is that the combination of the unambiguously racist, xenophobic, sexist, homo/transphobic, faux-populist, neoliberal Trump presidency, on the one hand, and the broad, cross-racial appeal of Senator Sanders' calls for a return to class-based progressive politics, on the other, have emboldened liberal race reductionists to lead with their unvarnished petit bourgeois political sensibilities.

In a 2017 appearance on the *Daily Show*, MSNBC's Joy-Ann Reid, for example, rejected the notion that economic anxiety contributed to Trump's resonance with some voters, and instead she traced his appeal to "values" rooted in long-standing ethnic/racial tribal identities. Like Coates, Reid criticized Democrats for wasting resources on efforts to woo Pabst Blue Ribbon–drinking, Archie Bunker–thinking blue-collar white voters who, according to Reid, have little interest in egalitarian economic policies. When host Trevor Noah asked Reid if Democrats might win future elections with platforms centered on universal economic policies from which blacks might benefit disproportionately, Reid responded by first asserting that Noah had described "the Bill Clinton strategy"—a formulation that works only if one forgets Bill Clinton's Republican-lite economic agenda—and then declaring that "on the race issue . . . what black people generally want is a reckoning."[4] In Reid's view, then, "black issues" are distinct from economic justice.

Ezra Klein echoed these sentiments in his July 2018 *Vox* article "White Threat in a Browning of America." According to Klein, Trumpism is a product of whites' discomfort with their shrinking share of the nation's overall population. Drawing from the work of political scientists, social psychologists and politicians, Klein argued that extant racial resentment was the source of the allegedly irrational economic anxieties articulated by many Trump supporters.[5] Like Reid, Klein not only ignores the implications of Trump's successes in Rustbelt states that Obama had previously won but also takes racial attitudes as a given. In other words, Klein—like so many others—looks past the fact that *both* parties have coalesced around explicitly racialized narratives about economic inequality that would necessarily foster racial tribalism.[6] Klein, moreover, has to ignore the economic precarity of voters in the industrial belts of states like Wisconsin, Michigan, Pennsylvania and Ohio, and the deserved resentment that many blue-collar Rustbelt voters had toward the Clintons.

The willingness of Coates, Klein, Reid and other race reductionists to accept the neoliberal agendas of Bill Clinton, Barack Obama and Hillary Clinton as realpolitik economic progressivism is a crucial tell. Indeed, their insistence that race operates independently of class serves a useful political function in a period marked by bipartisan disillusionment with the neoliberal consensus. Because liberal and even many left identitarians either firmly embrace or just take for granted neoliberalism's project of upward redistribution of wealth and the evisceration of the social safety net, they have few options but to cast racial disparities as evidence of *human*, rather than systemic, failures.

Put another way, racial reductionist explanations for mass incarceration, poverty, the wealth gap or even the 2016 presidential election shift attention from the political-economic underpinnings of inequality to frameworks centered on innate attitudes, disembodied identities and notions of privilege that are determined by skin color rather than wealth—the actual basis of power in a capitalist system.

Neoliberal identitarians ultimately reject historicist conceptions of race as an *ideology*, with a large cultural imprint,[7] that has long functioned to reify inequities organic to capitalism, because they see racism as an irrational drag on an otherwise rationally functioning market. Since, in their view, the political decisions that have deepened the ranks of losers in late-stage capitalism cannot be responsible for the high rates of black deprivation, neoliberal identitarians *must* mystify race—uncoupling it from the realm of social relations. And while this disposition leads race reductionists to the counter-solidaristic and, frankly, reprehensible conclusion that neoliberalism's non-black victims either deserve the miseries inflicted upon them or are merely collateral damage,[8] the implications of this project for poor and working-class African Americans are hardly positive. Indeed, reified notions of race and racial attitudes are the basis of the appeal of politically infeasible and misguided projects like reparations, and what has generated the swell of provocatively reactionary thought pieces and tweets that seek to explain why the minimum wage, Social Security and "Medicare for all" are supposedly racist.

Race reductionism's inability to provide effective solutions to material inequality is not confined to those who present political nonstarters like reparations as the only feasible fix to racial disparities. In fact, the seemingly "practical solutions" produced by those who insist on treating racism as if it operates independently of economic inequality often have proven track records of failure. Take, for example, Raj Chetty et al.'s recent meta-analysis of more than twenty-five years of US Census data. Intent on determining the influence of race and class over economic mobility, Chetty and his coauthors tracked long-term economic outcomes across two generations—parents and their offspring—of black, white, Hispanic, Asian and American Indian children. The researchers' analysis revealed three noteworthy findings. First, they observed persistent racial disparities across class lines. Second, the data revealed that black women, at all income levels, fared better than black men, while black women in some income groupings were actually marginally better off than white women. Third, though a racial gradient persisted across class lines, poor children of all races were more likely than their more affluent counterparts to grow up to be poor adults, while rich children of all races were more likely than their poor counterparts to become rich adults.[9]

A sober reading of the data should have affirmed the point that race and class are not separate but inextricably linked, as the study revealed the sway of both class and race over an individual's life chances. The researchers, however, stressed only the determinant role of race. Indeed, Chetty et al.'s recommendations reveal their disregard for the influence of economic class over what we generally refer to as racial disparities. Asserting that policies intended to "improve economic outcomes for a single generation"—including "cash transfer programs" and, curiously, "minimum wage increases"—might narrow the gap only temporarily, the researchers argue that "efforts that cut *within* neighborhoods and schools and improve environments for specific racial subgroups, such as black boys," would be more "effective in reducing the black-white gap." Chetty et al. thus proffered three specific remedies: "mentoring programs for black boys, efforts to reduce racial bias among whites, or efforts to facilitate social interaction across racial groups within a given area [including neighborhood integration]."[10] In other words, the researchers' recommendations centered largely on cultural tutelage.

As I've suggested, Chetty and his coauthors' proposals are hardly novel. In fact, the researchers' identification of cultural tutelage and interracial understanding as engines of black upward mobility sounds surprisingly similar to the failed racial uplift programs advanced by black civic organizations such as the National Urban League (NUL) in the years before the New Deal.[11] In the 1960s, War on Poverty programs such as Job Corps and Community Action, likewise, identified cultural tutelage as a vehicle for redressing racial inequities.[12]

Both Urban Leaguers and policymakers in the Johnson administration drew from models of ethnic group assimilation pioneered by the famed Chicago School of Sociology. Tracing issues like crime, juvenile delinquency, family dissolution and ethnic group conflict to social rather than biological processes, Chicago School concepts like ethnic cycle or interaction theory, social disorganization/reorganization and urban ecology were, in the early twentieth century, powerful tonics to counter bio-deterministic explanations for racial inequities. But because the Chicago School's race relations theories took for granted the logic of industrial capitalism, its sociological frameworks have tended to diminish political economy's crucial influence over racial disparities. Thus, the NUL's efforts to open employment and housing to blacks via vocational training and cultural tutelage—both of which were intended to foster mutually satisfying contact between the races—failed to uplift the race, in part, because racially tiered labor and housing markets enhanced capital's power and profits.[13] The War on Poverty, likewise, failed to end racial disparities because the Johnson administration's commitment to the fundamental distinctiveness of "black poverty" engendered policies that attempted to redress the failings of individuals and, perhaps, institutions—antidiscrimination legislation, job training programs and, of course, cultural tutelage—at the expense of any serious effort to address structural economic sources of inequality, such as the disproportionate impact of automation and Rustbelt deindustrialization on African Americans.[14]

Chetty et al. do not explicitly draw from Chicago School sociological frameworks; however, their conclusions are informed by sociologists and social psychologists who do draw from such models. But whatever the source of Chetty and his coauthors' commitment to a race reductionist interpretation of disparities, their disregard for the utility of government intervention in labor and housing markets lends itself to policies that would be of little value to most black boys, poor and working-class black men and women or, frankly, anyone who is not already reasonably well off.

Ultimately, Chetty et al.'s narrow focus on racial disparities precludes consideration of the political-economic underpinnings of black poverty. Specifically, the researchers make no mention of the devastating impact of public-sector retrenchment or the decline of the union movement on African Americans.[15] Because blacks have long been overrepresented among public-sector employees and trade unionists, revitalization of both the public sector and the union movement would yield disproportionate benefits for African American men and women alike. As I have already discussed, not only do unionized workers earn higher wages and are more likely to have benefits (both health care and pensions) than their nonunion counterparts, but collective bargaining agreements virtually eliminate race/sex pay gaps, making unionization among the most effective means of redressing disparities.[16]

Likewise, while the researchers dismiss the long-term benefits of "a minimum wage increase," a *living wage* would do much more to both reduce black poverty rates and enhance African Americans' ability to accumulate wealth than interracial friendships ever could. And though interactions "across racial lines" might, in the long run, undercut racial animus, it is not clear how mentoring for black boys or cultural competency training for white people would achieve common ground in the form of neighborhood integration—one of the researchers' stated goals. Indeed, since accelerating processes of rent-intensifying redevelopment (gentrification) in urban centers from the District of Columbia to the Bay Area have not swept out longtime black residents via formal racial bars but, instead, have *priced out* poor, working-class and even middle-class (black) homeowners and renters, wage supports—in the form of a living wage, unionization, cash transfers and expanding the public sector—along with affordable housing policies would likely be the most effective means of engendering the kind of racial amity that might blossom from interracial contact.

Of course, a living wage, unionization, a robust public sector and the creation of European-style public housing require the kind of public-good-oriented approach to governance that is at odds with neoliberalism's commitment to state support for market capitalism rather than the nation's citizenry.

The irony is that those who insist that we treat black poverty and racial inequality as if they have arisen independently of American political economy often encourage pursuit of remedies with a proven track record of failure for African Americans, at the expense of agendas that have actually worked for other racialized groups. As Bayard Rustin quipped to Black Powerites who naively embraced models of ethnic group political succession, the economic mobility that characterized the experiences of racialized white ethnics, like the so-called New Immigrants,[17] had far less to do with either the immigrants' cultural attributes or ethnic civic reformers' efforts to acculturate them than state intervention in labor and housing markets.[18] Indeed, the New Deal and postwar economic expansion did not simply enable hyphenated East European Americans, hyphenated Mediterranean Americans and Jews to ascend to the middle class; the opportunities the welfare state of yesteryear afforded these and other white ethnics also helped transform these once racialized groups into archetypical "Americans."[19]

Racial discrimination and America's bifurcated welfare state ensured that blacks would not share *equally* in the rewards of either the New Deal or the Keynesian consensus—though it is important that we not forget that many African Americans did benefit from the Wagner Act, the Work Projects Administration, the Civilian Conservation Corps, the Social Security Act, the GI Bill and so on. But the discriminatory administration of New Deal–era programs is not a case against universal employment, antipoverty and housing initiatives, any more than antidiscrimination legislation's failure to end racial disparities is a case against the importance of affirmative action, fair housing legislation and other such necessary initiatives. The point is that in the absence of state intervention in the operation of capitalist labor and housing markets, antidiscrimination legislation *alone* will be of little benefit to those African Americans who are crowded into underfunded public schools or barely regulated charter schools, who cannot afford college tuition, who graduate into a labor market characterized by depressed wages, who work for employers who not only are free to steal their meager wages but have no reason to provide benefits, and who earn too little to either rent a decent apartment or afford a healthy diet.

Had the Voting Rights Act of 1965 and Civil Rights Acts of 1964 and 1968 been passed thirty years earlier, then it is likely that we would not have the racial disparities that are before us today. In other words, had it been possible to pass these civil rights laws a generation earlier, blacks would likely have shared fully in the fruits of New Deal liberalism and the postwar Keynesian economic boom. But since the formal barriers to black upward mobility were dismantled a decade into what would eventually be known as deindustrialization and little more than a decade before the collapse of the Keynesian consensus, antidiscrimination legislation's efficacy was necessarily limited. And, of course, even if the Voting Rights and Civil Rights Acts had been passed a generation earlier, this would have done nothing to change the fortunes of the modern American middle and working classes; it would simply have diversified what has, despite its numbers, become a precarious segment of American society.

There is no question that too many Americans harbor racial prejudices; however, those of us who want to eliminate contemporary black poverty and inequality must insist on addressing the material sources of poor and even working-class

African Americans' disadvantage. Insistence on the distinctiveness of black poverty—traced to either ontological racism or the alleged cultural deficiencies of the black/brown poor themselves—has long lent itself to overlooking the fact that the pathways that white ethnics traveled from tenements to middle-class suburbs have steadily narrowed over the past half century.

The bottom line is that the fate of poor and working-class African Americans—who are unquestionably overrepresented among neoliberalism's victims—is linked to that of other poor and working-class Americans.[20] Our road to a more just society for African Americans and everyone else is obstructed, in part, by a discourse that declares the New Deal to be the root of all modern racial ills (despite the fact that the New Deal helped lay the foundation for the civil rights movement), that derides unions as racist (despite blacks' overrepresentation among unionists), that equates the "working class" with crusty old white men while equating entrepreneurialism with freedom and independence (like Black Belt slaveholders weren't petty capitalists) and that, ultimately, insists upon divorcing race from class.

ACKNOWLEDGMENTS

Writing books can require a little personal sacrifice and a lot of consideration from people in and on the periphery of one's life. I am grateful for the support and encouragement I have received from a great many friends, comrades, colleagues, former students and associates.

The seeds of this book were sown by an article I published in *Jacobin* magazine (August 2015), which was inspired both by a series of exchanges with former students Muriel Dorsey and Christopher Rauls and by a suggestion by Jay Arena. On the heels of the unexpected popularity of "Why Liberals Separate Race from Class," Verso Books' Andy Hsiao encouraged me to author a book-length treatment of the implications of liberals' long retreat from class analyses of inequality in favor of what I have termed "race reductionism."

Jacobin's Bhaskar Sunkara and Connor Kilpatrick and Verso Books' Asher Dupuy-Spencer offered invaluable assistance, shepherding the book through publication on an extremely tight production schedule.

Thomas Adams, Jay Arena, Chris Arnold, Roger Biles, Vivek

Chibber, Kyle Ciani, Todd Cronan, Bruce Dixon, Barbara J. Fields, Megan French-Marcelin, Heather Gautney, Briahna Joy Gray, Andrew Hartman, Cedric Johnson, Ross Kennedy, Walter Benn Michaels, Monica Noraian, James Oakes, Katrin Paehler, Adolph L. Reed Jr., Pascal Robert, Corey Robin, Dean Robinson, April Schultz, Robert Schultz, Preston Smith, Judith Stein, Joe Trotter, Rachel Watson and Cornel West all offered meaningful support, comments, insights or guidance.

I am indebted to research assistants Marc Hetzel, Diane Russeau-Pletcher and Wesley Ward for their diligence and friendship. Graduate student advisees Mark Adams, Emanuella Amoh, Lacey Brown, Brandon Henry and Trumaine Mitchell also provided valuable assistance.

The residency fellowship I was awarded by the John W. Kluge Center at the Library of Congress afforded me the time and resources to think through some of the issues with which this book is concerned, while the sabbatical Illinois State University granted me in spring 2017 gave me much-needed time to write.

My wife, Deirdre, has been a font of patience, kindness, consideration and happiness. She has not only helped smooth the sometimes rough edges of life but reminds me daily of the importance of never letting the bleakness of the historical moment eclipse life's joys.

Finally, my former colleagues at the Sewerage and Water Board of New Orleans (SWBNO), formerly the Orleans Parish Sewerage and Water Board, loom in the background of this and many other projects I have pursued over the years. As an adult, no single lived experience has had a more profound effect on my thinking about race and class than the year I spent working as a "permanent temporary employee." Prior to my time with SWBNO, I had temped as outsourced labor for a major oil company alongside a number of David Duke supporters. On the heels of this demoralizing experience, the months I worked as a dispatcher with the Sewerage and Water Board made clear that the bonds forged by shared experience *could* make an otherwise unsatisfying job very enjoyable. But even as the fond memories of my former coworkers at SWBNO continue to inspire, that experience also left little doubt that neither workplace camaraderie—as important as it is—nor supervisors, CEOs or public officials who "look like you" are capable of offsetting the toll of low wages, job insecurity and the absence of benefits like health insurance.

NOTES

Introduction: The Era of Race Reductionism

1 Alan Brinkley, "The New Deal and the Idea of the State," in *The Rise and Fall of the New Deal Order, 1930–1980*, ed. Steve Fraser and Gary Gerstle (Princeton: Princeton University Press, 1989), 98–100, 109–12; Brinkley, *The End of Reform: New Deal Liberalism in Recession and War* (New York: Vintage Books, 1996).

2 Nelson Lichtenstein, *State of the Union: A Century of American Labor* (Princeton: Princeton University Press, 2002), 30.

3 Ibid., 114–22.

4 Michael K. Brown, *Race, Money, and the American Welfare State* (Ithaca: Cornell University Press, 1999), 121–31; Mary Dudziak, *Cold War Civil Rights: Race and the Image of American Democracy* (Princeton: Princeton University Press, 2000), 82.

5 Julian E. Zelizer, "How Medicare Was Made," *New Yorker*, February 15, 2015, newyorker.com.

6 Steven Greenhouse, "Union Membership in US Fell to a 70-Year Low Last Year," *New York Times*, January 21, 2011, nytimes.com.

7 Economic Policy Institute, "The State of Working America: Key Numbers," stateofworkingamerica.org; Diana Hembree, "CEO Pay Skyrockets to 361 Times That of the Average Worker," *Forbes*, May 22, 2018, forbes.com; Drew Desilver, "For Most Workers, Real Wages Have Barely Budged for Decades," *Pew Research Center*, October 9, 2014, pewresearch.org; Heather Gautney, *Crashing the Party: From the*

Bernie Sanders Campaign to a Progressive Movement (New York: Verso Books, 2017), 19–31; Lichtenstein, *State of the Union*, 12–16. In 1968, for example, annual in-state tuition at University of Illinois, Urbana-Champaign, was $168; in 2018, tuition at UI-UC was about $16,000.

8 Bradford Richardson, "Clyburn: Sanders's Plan Would Kill Black Colleges," *The Hill*, February 21, 2016, thehill.com.

9 Annie Karni, "Clinton Race Speech Has Message for Sanders," *Politico*, February 16, 2016, politico.com. In the face of mounting criticism for her support of the 1994 omnibus Violent Crime Control and Law Enforcement Act, Secretary Clinton apologized (April 14, 2016, Democratic primary debate) for the "unintended consequences" of the crime bill that her husband had signed into law, but pivoted via a move that blended an act of contrition with "the Devil made me do it." Asserting that she had seen the crime act's "unfortunate impact on people's lives" firsthand, Clinton stated that she wanted to make sure that other "white people recognize that there is systemic racism" in the criminal justice system, as well as in employment and housing. Tessa Berenson, "Hillary Clinton Struggles to Defend 1994 Crime Act," *Time*, April 15, 2016, time.com; Clinton's tendency to attribute racial disparities in the criminal justice system to the "implicit bias" with which, she claimed, we are all afflicted, revealed her own reification of race/racism. While Clinton correctly called for retraining police officers to be aware of their own unrecognized prejudices, she mystified race/racism via biological metaphor, stating, in her so-called race speech in Philadelphia, that racism has been in our "DNA going back probably millennia." Given the ubiquitousness of DNA metaphors, the full implications of this statement may not be readily apparent to some readers. Race is not a biological category; it is a plastic ideology that, like all influential ideologies, has a cultural imprint. Ideologies (one's cognizance of social relations) and culture (a population's implicit understanding of social relations) are not products of biology, they are social constructions. To assert, then, that race/racism is encoded in our DNA is to imply that it is a *natural* phenomenon that is either resistant or impervious to the influence of proximate *social* influences. Clinton's formulation thus blurs the line between the social constructiveness of race (the contrivance of humans) and race/racism as a biological category (the product of nature). Dan Merica, "Hillary Clinton Talks Race: 'We All Have Implicit Biases,'" CNN, April 20, 2016, cnn.com.

10   Ta-Nehisi Coates, "Bernie Sanders and the Liberal Imagination," *Atlantic*, January 24, 2016, theatlantic.com; Ta-Nehisi Coates, "The Case for Reparations," *Atlantic*, June 2014.

11   Paul Richter, "Clinton Declares Affirmative Action Is 'Good for America,' " *Los Angeles Times*, July 20, 1995. While president Bill Clinton declared his support for affirmative action, he called for "mending it," rather than "ending it." Clinton's defense of affirmative action ceded unnecessary ground to conservative critics who had disingenuously equated affirmative action with quotas. Frank Dobbin, *Inventing Equal Opportunity* (Princeton: Princeton University Press, 2009), 102–3, 124–8.

12   Touré F. Reed, "Why I Voted for Nader in 2000 and Will Be Voting for Hillary Clinton in 2016," *The Nation*, October 6, 2016, thenation.com.

13   There are, of course, many reasons for Sanders's poor showing with black voters in 2016; name recognition is one of the more obvious ones. Today, Bernie Sanders is not only the most popular active politician in America, but, according to a 2017 Harvard-Harris poll, his popularity is actually highest among blacks. An August 2019 Pew poll likewise found that Sanders attracted a higher percentage of non-white supporters (51 percent) than Joe Biden (44 percent), Kamala Harris (41 percent) or Elizabeth Warren (29 percent). In the lead-up to the 2016 Democratic presidential primary race, however, few African Americans would have known Senator Sanders. Hillary Clinton, by contrast, not only benefited from Bill Clinton's (albeit undeserved) popularity with black voters, but the Clintons exerted significant influence over both the DNC and a large number of influential African American Democratic politicians. Symone Sanders, "It's Time to End the Myth that Black Voters Don't Like Bernie Sanders," *Washington Post*, September 12, 2017, washingtonpost.com; Carl Beijer, "The Quiet Death of the White Bernie Bro," *Jacobin*, August 17, 2019, jacobinmag.com.

14   Since President Obama bent over backwards to present himself as a "healer of racial wounds," I am sure some readers will reflexively object to characterizing him as a race reductionist. Obama did, indeed, avoid stark accounts of the effects of discrimination on racial disparities; nevertheless, his postracial presidency presumed that race, though not racism, was a major contributor to economic inequality. As I will discuss in Chapter 4, Obama drew heavily on underclass metaphors, which—by conflating culture with race—traced racial inequality to the

cultural deficiencies of poor African Americans themselves, uncoupling disparities from their material sources.

1. When Black Progressives Didn't Separate Race from Class

1   Bob Herbert, "Righting Reagan's Wrongs?," *New York Times*, November 13, 2007.

2   Frank Dobbin, *Inventing Equal Opportunity* (Princeton: Princeton University Press, 2009), 136–7.

3   Michael K. Brown, *Race, Money, and the American Welfare State* (Ithaca: Cornell University Press, 1999), *Whitewashing Race: The Myth of a Color-Blind Society* (Oakland: University of California Press, 2005); Michael Katz, *The Undeserving Poor: From the War on Poverty to the War on Welfare* (New York: Pantheon Books, 1989), *The "Underclass" Debate* (Princeton: Princeton University Press, 1992), *The Price of Citizenship: Redefining the American Welfare State* (New York: Henry Holt and Company, 2001); Jill Quadagno, *The Color of Welfare: How Racism Undermined the War on Poverty* (New York: Oxford University Press, 1996); Adolph L. Reed Jr, *Without Justice for All: The New Liberalism and Our Retreat from Racial Equality* (Boulder: Westview Press, 1999), *Class Notes: Posing as Politics and Other Thoughts on the American Scene* (New York: New Press, 2000), *Stirrings in the Jug: Black Politics in the Post-Segregation Era* (Minneapolis: University of Minnesota Press, 1999).

4   Theda Skocpol, *Social Policy in the United States: Future Possibilities in Historical Perspective* (Princeton: Princeton University Press, 1995); Paul Starr, "Civil Reconstruction: What to Do without Affirmative Action", *American Prospect* (Winter 1992); "Passion Memory, and Politics," *American Prospect* (Fall 1992), prospect.org; William J. Wilson, *The Declining Significance of Race: Blacks and Changing American Institutions* (Chicago: University of Chicago Press, 1980), *The Truly Disadvantaged: The Inner City, the Underclass, and Public Policy* (Chicago: University of Chicago Press, 1990).

5   Cedric G. Johnson, "Making Consumers and Criminals: The Postwar Urban Transformation and the Origins of Policing as We Know It," Unpublished Paper, February 20, 2018, University of Chicago Historical Capitalism Seminar Series.

6 See discussion in Chapter 4.

7 David Woolner, "Franklin and Eleanor, Human Rights," *Roosevelt Institute* (blog), February 5, 2010, rooseveltinstitute.org; "Party Realignment and the New Deal," *History, Art, and Archives: United States House of Representatives*, Office of Art and Archives, history.house.gov.

8 Nelson Lichtenstein, *State of the Union: A Century of American Labor* (Princeton: Princeton University , 79.

9 Harvard Sitkoff, *A New Deal for Blacks: The Emergence of Civil Rights as a National Issue: The Depression Decade* (New York: Oxford University Press, 2008).

10 Nelson Lichtenstein, *State of the Union: A Century of American Labor* (Princeton: Princeton University Press, 2002) 32.

11 Beth T. Bates, *Pullman Porters and the Rise of Protest Politics in Black America, 1925–1945* (Chapel Hill: UNC Press, 2001), 6–11.

12 Karl E. Klare, "Judicial Deradicalization of the Wagner Act and the Origins of Modern Legal Consciousness, 1937–1941," *University of Minnesota Law Review* 62(3): 296–8; Leon Keyserling, "The Wagner Act: Its Origin and Current Significance," *George Washington University Law Review* 26(2) (1960): 222–5.

13 Yellow-dog contracts threatened workers with termination if they attempted to either form or join labor unions.

14 Cheryl Greenberg, *"Or Does It Explode?": Black Harlem in the Great Depression* (New York: Oxford University Press, 1991), 121, 126–7; Winston McDowell, "Race and Ethnicity during the Harlem Jobs Campaign," *Journal of Negro History* 69(3/4) (1984): 138–9.

15 It should be noted that Hill was largely supportive of "Don't Buy Where You Can't Work;" he was, nonetheless, clear that such campaigns held the potential to legitimate white racial chauvinism in the workplace.

16 Paul Moreno, *From Direct Action to Affirmative Action* (Baton Rouge: LSU Press, 1997), 32–6.

17 Ibid., 41–52.

18 Pauli Murray, "The Right to Equal Opportunity in Employment," *California Law Review* 33(3) (1945): 388–433, 395.

19 Jonathan S. Holloway, *Confronting the Veil: Abram Harris Jr., E. Franklin Frazier, and Ralph Bunche, 1919–1941* (Chapel Hill: UNC Press, 2002), 6.

20 Patricia Sullivan, *Lift Every Voice: The NAACP and the Making of the Civil Rights Movement* (New York: New Press, 2009), 5, 18–24, 47–8.

21 Holloway, *Confronting the Veil*, 90–102.

22 A classic example of this conflict between the aims of the masses and the association's benefactors took place in Chicago in 1933, the same year as the Second Amenia Conference, when a member of the Chicago chapter of the NAACP executive board, Clement MacNeal, attempted to call a nationwide boycott of Sears Roebuck—whose board of directors was chaired by Lessing Rosenwald, brother of William Rosenwald, a major benefactor to the NAACP. The shoe department at Sears discriminated against black women in its Chicago locations. Despite popular support for MacNeal among black Chicagoans, Walter White reined in MacNeal at the urging of William Rosenwald.

23 Bates, *Pullman Porters and the Rise of Protest Politics in Black America*, 144–5.

24 Changes in Internal Revenue Service rules pertaining to nonprofit tax status prompted the NAACP to create the Legal Defense Fund. By the end of World War II, Marshall had hired five additional lawyers, including left-leaning Prentice Thomas and Marian Parry. See Bates, *Pullman Porters and the Rise of Protest Politics in Black America*, 142–5; Risa Goluboff, *The Lost Promise of Civil Rights* (Cambridge: Harvard University Press, 2007), 181–6.

25 Goluboff, *The Lost Promise of Civil Rights*, 200–5.

26 Ibid., 186, 198–210.

27 Touré F. Reed, *Not Alms but Opportunity: The Urban League and the Politics of Racial Uplift, 1910–1950* (Chapel Hill: UNC Press, 2008), 4–7.

28 Ibid., 112, 123.

29 Ibid., 122–4.

30 Ibid., 127.

31 Ibid., 124, 128–9.

32 Lester Granger, "Challenge to the Youth," 1938, 5–6, NAACP Papers, Vol. I, Box B15, Folder 7.

33 Reed, *Not Alms but Opportunity*, 88–90.

34 Erik S. Gellman, *Death Blow to Jim Crow: The National Negro Congress and the Rise of Militant Civil Rights Activism* (Chapel Hill: UNC Press, 2012), 12–14; Thomas J. Sugrue, *Sweet Land of Liberty: The Forgotten Struggle of Civil Rights in the North* (New York: Random House, 2008), 33–4.

35 Gellman, *Death Blow to Jim Crow*, 25–7; Sugrue, *Sweet Land of Liberty*, 33–4.

36 Gellman, *Death Blow to Jim Crow*, 30–62, 65–93.

37 Sugrue, *Sweet Land of Liberty*, 34.

38 Ibid., 38–9.

39 Bates, *Pullman Porters and the Rise of Protest Politics in Black America*, 151.

40 Paula F. Pfeffer, *A. Philip Randolph, Pioneer of the Civil Rights Movement* (Baton Rouge: LSU Press, 1990), 46–9.

41 Bates, *Pullman Porters and the Rise of Protest Politics in Black America*, 162–72; Pfeffer, *A. Philip Randolph*, 53–5.

42 Pfeffer, *A. Philip Randolph*, 90–3.

43 Ibid., 130–3.

44 Ibid., 234–9, 245.

45 Ibid., 240–8; William P. Jones, "The Unknown Origins of the March on Washington: Civil Rights Politics and the Black Working Class," *Labor* 7(3) (2010): 34–5.

46 Moreno, *From Direct Action to Affirmative Action*, 204.

47 Dobbin, *Inventing Equal Opportunity*, 34–5, 78–81, 83–93, 98–100, 102–6, 113–28, 130–2; Touré F. Reed, "Affirmative Action's Labor Roots," *Jacobin*, January 21, 2016, jacobinmag.com.

2. Oscar Handlin and the Conservative Implications of Postwar Ethnic Identitarianism

1 Some will likely equate my critical observation about the limits of "diversity" with opposition to affirmative action. Precisely because I know full well that racial and gender prejudice are still with us, I firmly embrace the need for antidiscrimination legislation and targeted recruitment endeavors—even if such initiatives *alone* are incapable of eliminating black poverty. My objection to "diversity," then, is not a veiled swipe at affirmative action, but rather it is a critique of contemporary diversity discourse.

In my view, diversity is a laudable end. However, over the past quarter-century the presumptions informing diversity have paralleled the "family-friendly" reactionary race science that AncestryDNA and 23andMe have helped mainstream. The pursuit of diversity had once presumed that interactions between individuals from "different backgrounds" would encourage majority/minority group members to recognize the absurdities of their prejudices, thereby discouraging stereotyping and discriminatory behavior. This is the conception of diversity that I firmly embrace. Though the dominant model of

diversity today likewise sees value in interactions between people
from "different backgrounds," it proceeds from the view that prejudice is owed to ignorance about "the other's" group-specific culture.
It likewise presumes that individual group members' unique cultural
traits, not simply their experiences, add value to the workplace and
classroom. The fundamental problem with the model of diversity
currently dominant is that it conflates culture with race. Racial
groups—which, since the twentieth century, have generally been
understood as continentally defined populations, Africans, Asians
and Europeans—might only be characterized by a common culture
if race is a biological or quasi-biological category rather than a social
construct. So, while affirmative action programs remain important
and should, therefore, be defended, the dominant diversity discourse
does "the Devil's work" insofar as it reifies race. Put another way,
diversity has come to promote inclusion not by challenging whites'
prejudices about black and brown people, but by promoting stereotyping—albeit with a positive spin—about people of color as the
basis for access. Readers who remain unsure about the point may
gain cringeworthy clarity by viewing clips of the "Miss Morello" and
"Craig" characters featured in *Everybody Hates Chris* and Donald
Glover's *Atlanta*, respectively.

2 The essentialist tendencies in intersectional analysis are well known.
Champions of intersectionality often insist that essentialist intersectional analyses are the product of sloppy application of the framework; however, if one reflects on Patricia Hill Collins's influential
"The Social Construction of Black Feminist Thought" (1989), this
defense is not entirely persuasive. Specifically, Collins's characterization of black feminist thought proceeds from the view that blacks
across the globe are bound together by a transhistorical Afrocentric
consciousness. While she argues that shared oppression wrought by
colonialism and slavery laid the groundwork for a common group-cul-
ture, this requires that one look past the differences in the colonial
systems, systems of slavery and postemancipation histories that,
along with geographical divides, would have exerted their own
particular influences over the disparate cultures and experiences of
slavery's descendants across the western hemisphere and, of course,
Africans. I make this point not to reduce intersectionality to one of
its earliest expressions as such or to one scholar. But it may well

be that practitioners who are guilty of essentialism may simply be following the path blazed by one of its pioneers, instead of going rogue. Patricia Hill Collins, "The Social Construction of Black Feminist Thought," *Signs* 14(4) (1989): 755–8.

Some have also suggested that there are two distinct intersectional camps—one rooted in Marxist critiques of capitalism and the other stemming from anti-left poststructuralism. If this is true, the second camp—which treats class as an identity group and uncouples race from time and place—is clearly dominant. See Bruce A. Dixon, "Looking Down that Deep Hole: Parasitic Intersectionality and Toxic Afro-Pessimism, Part 2 of 3," *Black Agenda Report*, February 1, 2018, blackagendareport .com; Sharon Smith, "A Marxist Case for Intersectionality," *Socialist Worker*, socialistworker.org.

3 See Chapter 4.

4 Cedric G. Johnson, "The Panthers Can't Save Us Now: Anti-policing Struggles and the Limits of Black Power," *Catalyst* 1(1) (2017): 57–85.

5 Oscar Handlin, *Race and Nationality in American Life* (New York: Doubleday Anchor Books, 1957), 152.

6 The Ford Foundation and Rockefeller Brothers Fund also provided financial support for Handlin's *The Newcomers*.

7 Oscar Handlin, *The Newcomers: Negroes and Puerto Ricans in a Changing Metropolis* (Cambridge: Harvard University Press, 1959), 117.

8 Peter J. Kellogg, "Civil Rights Consciousness in the 1940s," *The Historian* 42(1) (1979): 31–5.

9 Ibid., 25–6, 36–41; Eric Posner, "The Case against Human Rights," *Guardian*, December 4, 2014; Samuel Moyn, *Not Enough: Human Rights in an Unequal World* (Cambridge: Harvard University Press, 2018). There is little doubt that liberal efforts to cast racism as "un-American" were not without value, insofar as the characterization would help mobilize political opposition to Jim Crow and other formal barriers that had denied black Americans the full enjoyment of the rights and privileges of citizenship. But while white liberals' emphasis on racism's immorality focused on the misdeeds of white racists, recasting "the Negro problem" as "the white man's problem," as Gunnar Myrdal put it, this project shifted attention away from both race's historic function in American capitalism and the material—as opposed to psychological or cultural—costs of inequality for African Americans.

10 Nelson Lichtenstein, *State of the Union* (Princeton: Princeton University

Press, 2003), 114–18; Robert O. Self, *American Babylon: Race and the Struggle for Postwar Oakland* (Princeton: Princeton University Press, 2005), 7–9, 29–46.

11 Oscar Handlin, "Group Life within the American Pattern: Its Scope and Limits," *Commentary* (November 1949), 414–15.

12 Oscar Handlin, "The Goals of Integration," in "The Negro American—2," special issue, *Daedalus* 95(1) (1966): 268–86, 269.

13 Ibid., 271–2; Handlin, *Fire-Bell in the Night: The Crisis in Civil Rights* (Boston: Little, Brown and Company, 1964), 54–9.

14 Ibid., 272. It is worth noting that in 1949, Handlin had claimed that slavery "and the assumption of the abolitionists that there were no real differences between the Negroes and other Americans, long deprived this group of the opportunity to build a life of its own." Handlin, "Group Life within the American Pattern," 415–16.

15 Handlin, "The Goals of Integration," 283–4.

16 While Handlin rejected Moynihan's contention that the so-called crisis of the black family was rooted in slavery, he shared the view that family dissolution contributed to high rates of aberrant behavior among blacks. Specifically, Handlin claimed that the importance of female wage earners undermined the authority of black men/husbands, setting the stage for increased rates of sex and drug offenses among African Americans. Discrimination likewise, Handlin claimed, undermined blacks' commitment to thrift and education, further complicating blacks' acculturation. Handlin, *The Newcomers*, 74–8, 98–102.

17 Touré F. Reed, "The Educational Alliance and the Urban League in New York: Ethnic Elites and the Politics of Americanization and Racial Uplift, 1903–1932," in *Renewing Black Intellectual History: The Ideological and Material Foundations of African American Thought*, ed. Adolph Reed Jr. and Kenneth Warren (Boulder: Paradigm Publishers, 2009), 95–7.

18 Touré F. Reed, *Not Alms but Opportunity: The Urban League and the Politics of Racial Uplift, 1910–1950* (Chapel Hill: UNC Press, 2008), 19–26.

19 As historian Michael B. Katz has demonstrated, private charitable organizations had begun to press for government relief, sometimes reluctantly, even before the New Deal, as demand in industrial cities far outstripped the capacity of voluntary associations. Michael B. Katz, *In the Shadow of the Poorhouse: A Social Science History of Welfare in America* (New York: Basic Books, 1986), 158–62, 213.

20 Handlin, "The Goals of Integration," 281–2; Handlin, *Fire-Bell in the Night*, 64–7.

21 Handlin, *The Newcomers*, 86–90.

22 David Freund, "Marketing the Free Market: State Intervention and the Politics of Prosperity in Metropolitan America," in *The New Suburban History*, ed. Kevin Kruse and Thomas J. Sugrue (Chicago: University of Chicago Press, 2011), 22, 23–5. Robert O. Self's work on Oakland likewise draws attention to the intimate relationship between housing and economic policy on the creation of a middle-class white homeowner identity in the postwar era. See Robert O. Self, *American Babylon*. Both Eunice and George Grier's and Charles Abrams' contributions to the same special edition of *Daedalus*'s "The Negro American—2," in which Handlin's "Goals of Integration" appears, make plain that many of Handlin's contemporaries were also aware of the fact that the housing policies crafted by the real estate industry, business interests and the federal government were largely responsible for the racial divide between the nation's ghettoes and suburbs. Eunice and George Grier's "Beyond Equality" drew attention to the socioeconomic implications of FHA and VA mortgage policies that both privileged middle-class homeownership and established racial discrimination in housing as formal policy. Charles Abrams's "Housing Problem and the Negro" linked the 1965 Watts riot with the inequities of urban renewal policies that identified working class and poor black communities as impediments to economic growth. See Eunice and George Grier, "Equality and Beyond: Housing Segregation in the Great Society," *Daedalus* 95(1) (1966): 80–3; Charles Abrams, "The Housing Problem and the Negro," *Daedalus* 95(1) (1966): 64–76.

23 Handlin, "The Goals of Integration," 278–9.

24 Oscar and Lilian Handlin, *Liberty and Equality, 1920–1994* (New York: Harper Collins), 226–7, 278.

25 By the early 1960s, experience had prompted many state-level FEPCs to bar "unintentional discrimination" as well. Michael K. Brown et al., *Whitewashing Race: The Myth of a Color-Blind Society* (Berkeley: University of California Press, 2003), 166–70; Paul D. Moreno, *From Direct Action to Affirmative Action: Fair Employment Law and Policy, 1933–1972* (Baton Rouge: LSU Press, 1999), 203–10.

26 I will elaborate on this point in subsequent chapters, but the problem with affirmative action is not that it ran afoul of meritocracy or that it, and other antidiscrimination policies, bumped up against natural predilection.

The issue is that, for low-skilled black and brown workers, antidiscrimination policies—which did indeed help lay the foundation for a true black middle class—had been enacted about twenty-five years too late.

27 Pursuit of parity became more meaningful as federal action to address economic inequality through universal employment and income policies was preempted.

28 Walter Benn Michaels, "Race into Culture: A Critical Genealogy of Cultural Identity," *Critical Inquiry* 18(4) (1992): 655–85, 671, 682–5; Werner Sollors, "A Critique of Pure Pluralism," in *Reconstructing American Literary History*, ed. Sacvan Bercovitch (Cambridge: Harvard University Press, 1986), 273–9; historian Alice O'Connor's examination of culture of poverty discourse in the 1950s and 1960s highlights culturalists' ambivalence about the relationship between environment and group culture and behavior. Alice O'Connor, *Poverty Knowledge: Social Science, Social Policy, and the Poor in Twentieth-Century US History* (Princeton: Princeton University Press, 2001), 196–207.

29 Johnson, "The Panthers Can't Save Us Now."

30 Dean E. Robinson, *Black Nationalism in American Political Thought* (Cambridge: Cambridge University Press, 2001), 94; Johnson, "The Panthers Can't Save Us Now."

31 Robinson, *Black Nationalism in American Political Thought*, 93–4; Dean E. Robinson, "Black Power Nationalism as Ethnic Pluralism: Postwar Liberalism's Ethnic Paradigm in Black Radicalism," in *Renewing Black Intellectual History: The Ideological and Material Foundation of African American Thought*, ed. Adolph L. Reed Jr. and Kenneth W. Warren (Boulder: Paradigm Publishers, 2010), 198–9.

32 Robinson, *Black Nationalism in American Political Thought*, 93–4.

33 Stokely Carmichael and Charles Hamilton, *Black Power: The Politics of Liberation* (New York: Vintage Books, 1992), 44.

34 Bayard Rustin, "'Black Power' and Coalition Politics," *Commentary*, September 1966.

35 Robinson, *Black Nationalism and American Political Thought*, 94–6, 106; Johnson, "The Panthers Can't Save Us Now."

36 Rustin, "'Black Power' and Coalition Politics."

3. The Tragedy of the Moynihan Report

1 James T. Patterson, *Freedom Is Not Enough: The Moynihan Report and America's Struggle over Black Life from LBJ to Obama* (New York: Basic Books, 2010), xii.

2 Ibid., xiii–xv, 68–71.

3 Stack claimed that under/unemployed fathers were often still in the picture and single mothers frequently plugged into effective kinship networks.

4 See my discussion of Laura Carper later in the chapter.

5 William Julius Wilson, *The Truly Disadvantaged: The Inner City, the Underclass, and Public Policy* (Chicago: University of Chicago Press, 1987), 4.

6 Patterson, *Freedom Is Not Enough*, xvi, 149–57.

7 Ibid., 213.

8 Daniel P. Moynihan, "The Negro Family: The Case for National Action," in *The Moynihan Report and the Politics of Controversy*, ed. Lee Rainwater and William A. Yancey (Cambridge: MIT Press, 1967), 48–9.

9 Ibid., 52–60.

10 Daniel P. Moynihan, US Senate, Committee on Finance, The Work and Responsibility Act of 1994, July 13, 1994, transcript, 12.

11 Moynihan, *The Negro Family*, 52–5, 58, 61–4.

12 Ibid., 93.

13 Ibid.

14 Daniel P. Moynihan, "Employment, Income, and the Ordeal of the Negro Family," in "The Negro American" special issue, *Daedalus* 94(4) (1965): 745–70, 748, 751–4, 758.

15 Ibid., 764–5.

16 Ibid., 764, 768–9.

17 Laura Carper, "The Negro Family and the Moynihan Report," in *The Moynihan Report and the Politics of Controversy*, 469–70. Carper's contribution to the Rainwater and Yancey collection was originally published in *Dissent*, March–April 1966.

18 Alice O'Connor, *Poverty Knowledge: Social Science, Social Policy and the Poor in Twentieth-Century US History* (Princeton: Princeton University Press, 2001), 148–9.

19 Ibid., 146–9.

20 Ibid., 149–51.

21 Judith Stein, *Running Steel, Running America: Race, Economic Policy, and the Decline of Liberalism* (Chapel Hill: UNC Press, 1998), 71–3, 77–8; Judith Russell, *Economics, Bureaucracy, and Race: How Keynesians Misguided the War on Poverty* (New York: Columbia University Press, 2003), 35–6, 40.

22 Stein, *Running Steel*, 70; Russell, *Economics, Bureaucracy, and Race*, 23–5.

23 Robert J. Lampman, "The Low-Income Population and Economic Growth," in US Congress, Joint Economic Committee, *Study Papers* (Washington, 1959), 26–31.

24 Carl M. Brauer, "Kennedy, Johnson, and the War on Poverty," *Journal of American History* 69(1) (1982): 98–119, 104–6; *The Annual Report of the Council of Economic Advisers* (Washington, 1964), 54.

25 Brauer, "Kennedy, Johnson, and the War on Poverty,"108.

26 Daniel P. Moynihan, "The Professionalization of Reform," *The Public Interest* 1 (1965): 6–16, 10.

27 Ibid., 10–11.

28 Because Moynihan was assistant secretary of labor, some might be inclined to conflate Secretary of Labor Wirtz's and Moynihan's positions on employment. As Samuel Merrick, assistant to the secretary of labor (1962–8) pointed out, however, Moynihan and Wirtz had a complicated if not antagonistic relationship. And while Moynihan did call for "full employment," the meaning of full employment, as I will elaborate on later, was contested—it did not necessarily equate with public works. Indeed, Moynihan's emphasis on the distinctiveness of black poverty, his indifference to the consequences of transformation of the American economy, and his technocratic calls for tweaks to service provision targeting poor people placed him more in line with the CEA's tax-and-spend antipoverty strategies rather than Wirtz's calls for redistributive policies such as public works. Michael L. Gillette, *Launching the War on Poverty: An Oral History* (New York: Oxford University Press, 2010), 108.

29 Charles C. Killingsworth, *Jobs and Income for Negroes* (*Policy Papers in Human Resources and Industrial Relations*), Joint Publication of the Institute of Labor and Industrial Relations (University of Michigan and Wayne State University, 1968): 35–7.

30 Ibid., 35.

31 Ibid., 36–9.

32 Ibid., 64–71, 80–1.

33 Ibid., 59–62, 71–8.

34 Ibid., 50.

35 Bayard Rustin, "From Protest to Politics," *Commentary* 39 (February 1965): 25–32, 26.

36 Michael Harrington, "The Politics of Poverty," *Dissent* 12 (1965): 416.

37 Rustin, "From Protest to Politics," 2–3.

38 Harrington, "The Politics of Poverty," 419–22.

39 Ibid., 424–6.

40 Rustin, "From Protest to Politics," 4–5. Rustin's contention in *Commentary* was the same as that staked out by Randolph at the 1963 March on Washington. "Yes, we want a Fair Employment Practice Act," Randolph declared at the rally, "but what good will it do if profit-geared automation destroys the jobs of millions of workers black and white?" Algernon Austin, "The Unfinished March: An Overview," Economic Policy Institute, June 18, 2013, epi.org.

41 Paul Le Blanc and Michael Yates, *A Freedom Budget for All Americans: Recapturing the Promise of the Civil Rights Movement in the Struggle for Economic Justice Today* (New York: Monthly Review Press, 2013), 90–6.

42 Ibid., 110–17.

43 Harrington, "The Politics of Poverty," 414; Alan Brinkley's *The End of Reform* provides a comprehensive analysis of the tension between regulatory and fiscal approaches to economic stewardship during the New Deal and World War II. Alan Brinkley, *The End of Reform: New Deal Liberalism in Recession and War* (New York: Vintage Books, 1995).

44 Russell, *Economics Bureaucracy, and Race*, 6–10, 151–7; Stein, *Running Steel, Running America*, 70–6.

45 Patterson, *Freedom Is Not Enough*, 167.

46 John Arena, "Why Does Angela Glover Blackwell Hate Public Housing? The Ideological Foundations of Public Housing Dismantlement in the United States and New Orleans," in "The Report Moynihan and the Crescent City: Culturalism and Katrina in New Orleans," ed. Touré F. Reed, *nonsite.org* 17 (2015), nonsite.org.

47 Even many contemporary critics of the Moynihan Report have accepted the narrow parameters of poverty discourse established by institutional structuralism. Historian Daniel Geary, for example, recently argued that Moynihan's focus on black social pathology deflected attention from institutional racism. This was certainly a position that some critics of the Moynihan Report staked out in the 1960s. Nevertheless, there are two problems with this charge. First, as his defenders correctly argue,

Moynihan identified racism as the ultimate source of poverty and, by extension, the tangle of pathology that threatened to impede black progress. Second, as Killingsworth and Rustin argued, institutional racism, though real and relevant, was not the principal cause of black poverty in the 1960s, nor is it today. The tendency to criticize Moynihan for his racial insensitivity or even racism (and, to be clear, Geary does not cast Moynihan as a racist) is no less illustrative of the hegemony of what we know today as neoliberalism than are defenses of Moynihan that presume his identification of racism as the root cause of poverty *fully* insulates him against the charge of victim blaming. Both perspectives look past the centrality of deindustrialization, the decline of the union movement and an intensifying attack on social wage protections (particularly in the context of the legacy of housing discrimination) as sources of persistent poverty among African Americans. Daniel Geary, "The Moynihan Report Is Turning 50. Its Ideas on Black Poverty Were Wrong Then and Are Wrong Now," *In These Times*, June 30, 2015, inthesctimes.com.

4. Obama and Coates: Postracialism's and Post-postracialism's Yin-Yang Twins of Neoliberal Benign Neglect

1 Ta-Nehisi Coates, "The Case for Reparations," *Atlantic*, June 2014, theatlantic.com.

2 Larry DeWitt, "The Decision to Exclude Agricultural and Domestic Workers from the 1935 Social Security Act," *Social Security Bulletin* 70(4) (2010): 49–68, 52–3.

3 Ibid., 52.

4 Lee Alston and Joseph P. Ferrie, "Labor Costs, Paternalism, and Loyalty in Southern Agriculture: A Constraint on the Growth of the Welfare State," *Journal of Economic History* 45(1) (1985): 95–117, 99–101.

5 DeWitt, "The Decision to Exclude Agricultural and Domestic Workers from the 1935 Social Security Act," 52–5.

6 Coates, "The Case for Reparations."

7 David Freund, "Marketing the Free Market: State Intervention and the Politics of Prosperity in Metropolitan America," in *The New Suburban History*, ed. Kevin Kray and Thomas J. Sugrue (Chicago University of

Chicago Press, 2011), 19–22.

8 Robert O. Self, *American Babylon: Race and the Struggle for Postwar Oakland* (Princeton: Princeton University Press, 2005), 7–9, 29–46.

9 Freund, "Marketing the Free Market," 15–19, 20–3.

10 Lisa Hsiao, "Project 100,000: The Great Society's Answer to Military Needs in Vietnam," *Vietnam Generation* 1(2) (1989): 15.

11 Frank Dobbin, *Inventing Equal Opportunity* (Princeton: Princeton University Press, 2009), 140–1.

12 Coates, "The Case for Reparations."

13 Algernon Austin, "The Unfinished March: An Overview," *Economic Policy Institute*, June: 2013, epi.org.

14 Judith Stein, *Running Steel, Running America: Race, Economic Policy and the Decline of Liberalism* (Chapel Hill: UNC Press, 1998), 79–83.

15 Although Coates and a long list of activists and pundits have characterized class-oriented redistributive policies of the sort proposed by Senator Bernie Sanders in his 2016 and 2020 bids for the Democratic presidential nomination as "the same 'a rising tide lifts all boats' thinking" that has failed black Americans since the War on Poverty, this is a total mischaracterization of the metaphor. Indeed, the "rising tide" metaphor—which was a New England Chamber of Commerce slogan that President Kennedy's speechwriter, Ted Sorensen, co-opted—was wed to the Kennedy and Johnson administrations' case *against* redistributive economic policies, in favor of commercial Keynesianism's more conservative growth agenda.

16 I resisted the urge to count the number of times Coates references "the body," "bodies" or "plunder" in his three major essays; however, in a version of this chapter that appeared in the journal *Catalyst* I indicated that African American lawyer and labor organizer R. L. Stephens reported that Coates uses "the body" or "bodies" more than 300 times in his 150-page best seller *Between the World and Me*. I have since gone through *Between the World and Me* myself and found that Coates refences "the body" or "bodies" nearly 200 times. R. L. Stephens, "The Birthmark of Damnation and the Black Body," *View Point Magazine*, May 17, 2017, viewpointmag.com.

17 Ta-Nehisi Coates, "Why Precisely Is Bernie Sanders against Reparations," *Atlantic*, January 19, 2016, theatlantic.com; Ta-Nehisi Coates, "Bernie Sanders and the Liberal Imagination," *Atlantic*, January 24, 2016.

18 As late as 1979, nearly a quarter of black workers in the United States

held jobs in manufacturing. Today, fewer than 10 percent are employed in manufacturing.

19 In 1983, 31.7 percent of all black workers belonged to a union or were covered by a union contract, compared to 22.2 percent of white workers. By 2015, the percentage had fallen to 14.2 percent and 12.5 percent for black and white workers respectively. Cherrie Bucknor, "Black Workers, Unions, and Inequality," Center for Economic Policy and Research, cepr.net; Ben Zipperer, "African American Workers Are Hurt More by the Decline in Union and Manufacturing Jobs," Washington Center for Equitable Growth, March 31, 2016, equitablegrowth.org.

20 Marie Gottschalk, *Caught: The Prison State and the Lockdown of American Politics* (Princeton: Princeton University Press, 2015), 132–5.

21 Oliver Laughland, "Justice Denied: The Human Toll of America's Public Defender Crisis," *Guardian*, September 7, 2016, theguardian.com.

22 John M. Eason, "Prison Building Will Continue Booming in Rural America," *Salon*, March 15, 2017, salon.com; Gottschalk, *Caught*, 31–4.

23 Leah Sakala, "Breaking Down Mass Incarceration in the 2010 Census: State-by-State Race/Ethnicity," Prison Policy Initiative, May 28, 2014, prisonpolicy.org/reports/rates.html.

24 Ta-Nehisi Coates, "My President Was Black: A History of the First African American White House—and What Came Next," *Atlantic*, January/February 2017, theatlantic.com.

25 Ibid.

26 Coates, *Between the World and Me* (New York: Spiegel & Grau, 2015), 79–85.

27 Coates, "My President Was Black."

28 David Madland and Karla Walter, "The Employee Free Choice Act 101," Center for American Progress action, March 11, 2009, american-progressaction.org.

29 Steven Mufson and Tom Hamburger, "Labor Union Officials Say Obama Betrayed Them in Health-care Rollout," *Washington Post*, January 31, 2014, washingtonpost.com.

30 David Moberg, "8 Terrible Things about the Trans Pacific Partnership," *In These Times*, December 16, 2015, inthesetimes.com.

31 Mufson and Hamburger, "Labor Union Officials Say Obama Betrayed Them in Health-care Rollout."

32 Libby Nelson, "'Why We Voted for Donald Trump': David Duke Explains the White Supremacist Charlottesville Protest," *Vox*, August 12, 2018.

33 Jessica Taylor, "The Counties That Flipped from Obama to Trump, in 3 Charts," NPR Politics, November 15, 2016, npr.org.

34 Sean McElwee and Jason McDaniel, "Fear of Diversity Made People More Likely to Vote Trump," *Nation*, March 14, 2017, thenation.com.

35 Coates, "My President Was Black."

36 Adolph Reed Jr., *Stirrings in the Jug: Black Politics in the Post-Segregation Era* (Minneapolis: University of Minnesota Press, 1999), 179–80.

37 William Julius Wilson, *The Truly Disadvantaged: The Inner City, the Underclass, and Public Policy* (Chicago: University of Chicago, 1987), 4, 16–18.

38 "A Visit with Bill Clinton: The Conflict between the 'A Student' and the 'Pol,'" *Atlantic*, October 1992, theatlantic.com.

39 "Barack Obama's Keynote Address at the 2004 Democratic National Convention," *PBS NewsHour*, July 27, 2004, pbs.org.

40 Transcript: Barack Obama's, Speech on Race," NPR, March 18, 2008, npr.org.

41 "Obama's Father's Day Remarks," *New York Times*, June 15, 2008, nytimes. com.

42 When explaining his decision to endorse Obama in December 2007, for example, not only did Senator John Kerry say that Obama showed "young blacks in America [and] disaffected young people" generally what they could achieve if they "work[ed] at it," but he went on to say in that same interview, "Barack Obama can say things to African American leaders that a white president just can't say." Journalist Matt Bai's flawed "Is Barack Obama the End of Black Politics?" observed that Obama's postracialism hinged on the combination of his willingness to both assure white voters that he did not have a chip on his shoulder—in contrast to the first post–Voting Rights Act wave of black elected officials—and his related disposition to publicly upbraid poor blacks. Likewise, in the wake of Obama's so-called race speech and Father's Day address, political commentator Glenn Greenwald praised the presidential candidate for having the courage to lecture black people about their own cultural deficiencies and then went on to urge Obama to step up these efforts. See "Transcript: Sen." John Kerry Discusses Obama Endorsement, ABC News, December 13, 2007, abcnews.go.com; Matt Bai, "Is Obama the End of Black Politics?" *New York Times Magazine*, August 6, 2008, nytimes.com; Glenn Greenwald, Obama's Rightward Iack?," interview by Tom Ashbrook, *On Point*,

July 10, 2008, onpoint.legacy.wbur.org.

43 Questions about his racial authenticity had dogged Obama during his 2000 primary challenge for Bobby Rush's seat in the US House of Representatives. Rush was not just a four-term incumbent but also a former member of the Student Nonviolent Coordinating Committee (SNCC) and the Black Panther Party (BPP)—an icon of the civil rights movement. Though Obama won the white vote handily, Rush trounced him in the primary by a two-to-one margin. In Illinois's majority-black first congressional district, the Ivy League–educated African American state senator from Hawaii lacked the bona fides to unseat Rush, who quipped at the time: "Barack Obama went to Harvard and became an educated fool. Barack is a person who read about the civil rights protests and thinks he knows all about it." Janny Scott, "In 2000, a Streetwise Veteran Schooled a Bold Young Obama," *New York Times*, September 9, 2007, nytimes.com.

44 Paul Krugman, "Stimulus Arithmetic (Wonkish but Important)," *New York Times*, January 9, 2009, krugman.blogs.nytimes.com.

45 Amanda Terkel, "Bachmann Blames President Clinton, 'Blacks,' and 'Other Minorities' for Current Financial Crisis," *Think Progress*, September 26, 2008, thinkprogress.org.

46 Ariel Colonomos and Andrea Armstrong, "German Reparations to the Jews after World War II: A Turning Point in the History of Reparations," in *The Handbook of Reparations*, ed. Pablo De Greiff (New York: Oxford University Press, 2006), 290–3.

47 In lieu of contextual analysis, Coates describes Royall's successful 1783 bid for reparations as a rare moment in which the pangs of conscience trumped white Americans' racist disregard for black bodies. "At the time [of the Royall verdict], black people in America had endured more than 150 years of enslavement," he says, "and the idea that they might be owed something in return was, if not the national consensus, at least not outrageous." Coates characterizes West Germany's decision to make restitution to Jewish Holocaust victims and Israel as the act of a people whose desire to return to the ranks of the civilized world afforded them an opportunity for collective healing. "Reparations payments could not make up for the murder perpetrated by the Nazis," Coates says, "but they did launch Germany's reckoning with itself, and perhaps provided a road map for how a great civilization might make itself worthy of the name." See Coates, "The Case for Reparations."

48 Ibid.

49 Coates, *Between the World and Me*, 16–17; Ta-Nehisi Coates, "Beyond the Code of the Streets," *New York Times*, May 3, 2013, nytimes.com.

50 In his review of *Between the World and Me*, conservative commentator David Brooks indicated that he found Coates's articulation of black "rage" revelatory. Brooks was not altogether sure what to make of all of Coates's assessments of black life, partly because Coates appeared, as Brooks put it, committed to being misunderstood; nevertheless, Coates's characterization of black dysfunctionality resonated with Brooks. Brooks likewise offered a telling circumspection about Coates's historical analysis. Specifically, Brooks found Coates's allegation of "causation between the legacy of lynching and some guy's decision to commit a crime" unpersuasive. It is not surprising that David Brooks would criticize Coates for failing to consider how individual choice informs outcomes, but Coates's tendency to reduce all systems of inequality to a one-size-fits-all racism leaves him susceptible to this type of critique. David Brooks, "Listening to Ta-Nehisi Coates while White," *New York Times*, July 17, 2015, nytimes.com.

At the other end of the political spectrum, economist Robert Cherry cites Coates's *The Beautiful Struggle* as evidence that poverty alone is not responsible for the disproportionately large number of black perpetrators of violent crimes. Cherry is clear that poverty is the principal contributor to nonviolent crimes and a contributor to violent crimes across racial lines. However, he attributes the higher rates of violent crimes among blacks—when compared with poor whites and Latinos—to a subculture of violence that has taken hold of a stratum of young black men. Cherry ultimately draws from Coates to buttress a Moynihan-like narrative chastening those progressives who, in the 2016 election season, called for an economic response to black poverty. Ironically, Cherry used Coates to place Hillary Clinton's 1994 super-predator remarks in (what he believed to be the appropriate) context. When one considers the role that underclass ideology has played in stifling attempts to redress material sources of inequality, Cherry's use of Coates offers insights into the inadequacies of Coates's framework. Robert Cherry, "Race and Rising Violent Crime," *Real Clear Policy*, February 16, 2017, realclearpolicy.com.

51 Touré F. Reed, "Affirmative Action's Labor Roots," *Jacobin*, January 21, 2016, jacobinmag.com.

Conclusion: Race Reductionism and the Path to Precarity for All but a Diverse Few

1   Jeb Bush applauded President Trump's nomination of Neil Gorsuch, his brother George W. Bush lobbied behind the scenes for Brett Kavanaugh—who worked in his administration—during his contentious nomination, and Ted Cruz voted to confirm both Gorsuch and Kavanaugh. Michelle Mark, "Jeb Bush on Trump: I Told You So," *Business Insider*, May 20, 2017, businessinsider.com; Daniel Lippman, "Exclusive: Bush Reaffirms Support for Kavanaugh," *Politico*, September 18, 2018, politico.com.

2   Jamil Smith, "Elizabeth Warren's New Plan to Close the Racial Wealth Gap," *Rolling Stone*, June 14, 2019, rollingstone.com; Rebecca Safier, "Student Loans Weigh the Heaviest on Black and Hispanic Students," Student Loan Hero, September 17, 2018, studentloanhero.com.

3   Safier, "Student Loans Weigh the Heaviest on Black and Hispanic Students."

4   *The Daily Show* with Trevor Noah, August 29, 2017, cc.com.

5   Ezra Klein, "White Threat in a Browning America," *Vox*, July 30, 2018, vox.com.

6   See my critique of Sean McElwee and Jason McDaniel in Chapter 4. See also Touré F. Reed, "The Ties that Divide: How Bipartisan Identitarianism Works for the Boss and Against Citizen and Non-Citizen Workers," *Common Dreams*, January 22, 2018, commondreams.org.

7   I have made a point of stressing that race, like all influential ideologies, has cultural significance because most people who are racists are not ideologues, but they have only folk understandings of the material hierarchies that racial ideology buttresses. So, while Charles Murray, his coauthor Richard Herrnstein and their hero J. Philippe Rushton contemplated the hierarchical functionality of race as part of an explicitly antidemocratic political-economic project, most racists, having only an intuitive sense of "race," do not understand themselves to be embracing an ideology whose function is to abstract inequities from the human, economic processes that generate them. I am compelled to emphasize this point as I suspect that some who read historicist accounts of racial ideology find them dissatisfying because few of us have ever known any racists who would articulate their prejudices in terms that reveal their awareness of the hegemonic function of "races."

This reality is the fertile ground in which the phrase "race takes on a life of its own" takes root.

The fact that most racists would not be capable of articulating racism's functionality in material terms, even as they reflexively embrace the concept, is not evidence of race's metaphysical qualities, it is the work of cultural hegemony. Many of those who insist on divorcing race from class seem to conflate—unwittingly or not—the culturally informed reflexes of our racist neighbors, coworkers, supervisors, classmates, etc. with the reasoned projects of ideologues like Murray, Herrnstein and Rushton. But if race's historical job is to reify material hierarchies, then no one should expect "racists" to explicitly articulate race in those terms. Even so, if one reads between the lines of historically contingent, cultural understandings of what race is, the concept's functionality as a vehicle for reifying material hierarchies is plain. Indeed, every racist coworker, classmate, teacher, neighbor, supervisor, etc. whom I have ever known has presumed African Americans to be some combination of lazy, unintelligent, hedonistic, irresponsible and impulsive. These are, of course, the very same characteristics, stereotypes, that many people apply to poor people—including whites. This is also the prejudicial basis for the backhanded compliment "you're not *really* black" to which so many well-educated, articulate and/or prosperous African Americans are all too often subjected.

8 Often enough, the contention that white victims of police brutality, mass incarceration or man-made disasters have either deserved their fate or were merely casualties in an assault on black Americans is only implied. Take, for example, the ubiquitous and erroneous assertion that police shootings targeting unarmed men and women "do not happen to white people" and the similar tendency to characterize the poisoning of the citizens of Flint—at the hands of Michigan governor Rick Snyder and his black henchman, former Flint city manager Darnell Earley—as "environmental racism," rather than calling this horrific act what it was— the human toll of neoliberalism's undemocratic and inhumane assault on the public sector. Some individuals do, however, explicitly make this case. For example, though there is much to recommend in Michelle Alexander's *The New Jim Crow*, Alexander explicitly describes the white victims of mass incarceration as "collateral damage." Michelle Alexander, *The New Jim Crow: Mass Incarceration in the Age of Colorblindness* (New York: New Press, 2012), 205; see also Josiah Rector, "Neoliberalism's

Deadly Experiment," *Jacobin*, October 16, 2016, jacobinmag.com.

9 Raj Chetty, Nathaniel Hendren, Maggie R. Jones and Sonya R. Porter, "Race and Economic Opportunity in the United States: An Intergenerational Perspective," National Bureau of Economic Research, Working Paper 24441, March 2018: 1–4, 21–3, 31–2, nber.org/papers/w24441.

10 Ibid., 42.

11 In its first two decades of operation, the National Urban League embarked on an antiracist project that set out to promote mutually satisfying contact between the races via cultural tutelage and job training for black workers and tenants. The NUL presumed that evidence of proficient black workers and respectable black tenants would disabuse white employers, trade unionists, homeowners and landlords of their irrational racial prejudices, thereby opening access to employment and housing from which African Americans had been barred in the era of eugenics and Jim Crow. Prior to the New Deal, the league's strategy paid only occasional dividends for a comparatively small number of disproportionately middle-class African Americans. Touré F. Reed, *Not Alms but Opportunity: The Urban League and the Politics of Racial Uplift, 1910–1950* (Chapel Hill: University of North Carolina Press, 2008).

12 See discussion in Chapter 3.

13 It is worth noting that NUL leaders such as T. Arnold Hill and Lester Granger would ultimately embrace the New Deal's efforts to reform labor markets, precisely because they understood that voluntarist, culturalist approaches to racial inequality were incapable of redressing the roots of black joblessness. This is much the same reason that the more conservative Whitney Young would embrace S-1937 in the early 1960s. So, while the NUL never jettisoned its culturalist understanding of inequality, its leadership, nonetheless, understood the value of state intervention in labor and housing markets during the Keynesian consensus.

14 See discussion in Chapters 3 and 4.

15 Though the researchers report that black and white children in the "industrial Midwest" experienced the lowest rates of upward mobility, they do not explore the region's economic history. The Rustbelt has been hemorrhaging industrial jobs for about as long as the children who are the subject of this study—individuals born between 1978 and 1983—have been alive. The loss of well-paying *unionized* blue-collar work would have been especially devastating to black men, a group that is of particular concern to Chetty and his coauthors. Likewise,

for more than a decade, public-sector employees have experienced significant setbacks in Michigan, Indiana, Wisconsin and, to a lesser extent, Illinois.

16 See discussion in Chapter 4.

17 We have lost sight of the fact that at the turn of the twentieth century, Americans had generally perceived East Europeans, Mediterranean Europeans and Jews to be racially distinct from "Old Stock" Americans who were descendants of Northern Europeans. In fact, not only did these groups face racial discrimination in the workplace and in housing, but eugenicists and nativists warned that Jews and immigrants from eastern and southern Europe were of such inferior racial stock that their continued immigration to the United States posed a threat to American society. This would lead to the near total exclusion of immigration from southern and eastern Europe via the Immigration Restriction Acts of 1921 and 1924. Edwin Black, *War against the Weak: Eugenics and America's Campaign to Create a Master Race* (New York: Four Walls Eight Windows, 2003), 185–9, 192–9, 202–5.

To be sure, the New Immigrants did not face the rigid racial barriers that confronted African Americans—so, I am not repackaging Oscar Handlin's "last immigrant" thesis. They did, however, face intense racial discrimination. Moreover, as should be made evident by the so-called one-drop rule, the advantages white ethnics possessed over blacks were owed less to some abstract notion of "white skin privilege" than the fact that they—in contrast to African Americans—had never been a major source of bound labor in this country. Indeed, post-emancipation racial ideology was tied directly to the South's labor force needs. Disfranchised African Americans remained a vital part of the Southern agricultural economy through the mid-twentieth century, which solidified business interests', philanthropists' and politicians' commitments to claims of black racial inferiority. According to historians such as Judith Stein, then, it is not mere coincidence that the civil rights movement achieved its major successes in the South in a moment marked by the declining importance of African American agricultural labor to the region's economy. Southern business elites' commitment to Jim Crow was attenuated by both the invention of the mechanical cotton picker and their desire to attract manufacturers, many of them government contractors, to the region during a moment, the Cold War, in which Jim Crow undercut the United States' international standing. Judith Stein, *Running Steel,*

Running America: Race, Economic Policy, and the Decline of Liberalism (Chapel Hill: UNC Press, 1998), 313.

18	Bayard Rustin, "'Black Power' and Coalition Politics," *Commentary*, September 1966.

19	Racialized ethnic divisions among white ethnics have not only faded over time but—contrary to the presumptions driving ethnic pluralism—have more and more been brushed aside by shared residential and educational experiences. Indeed, most of my college students with obvious Mediterranean or East European last names not only mispronounce their surnames but—if they are fourth- or fifth-generation Americans, as most are—also either describe their ethnic European heritage as mixed or just cannot say "what they are" with any certainty. In other words, their identities as Italian American, Greek American, Polish American, Lithuanian American, Irish American, etc. are often eclipsed by their identities as white people from Oak Park, Naperville, Oak Brook, Bridgeport, Joliet, etc. And if this were not the case, then there would be no market for the pseudoscientific, fundamentally racist—in the true sense of the word—parlor-trick services provided by AncestryDNA and 23andMe.

20	In 2016, blacks accounted for about 40 percent of inmates, while whites and Latinos comprised nearly 60 percent of the inmate population. As political scientist Cedric Johnson notes, in 2015 blacks accounted for about 28 percent of those murdered at the hands of police officers, while whites and Latinos account for about 70 percent of such individuals. Roughly 20 percent of blacks live in poverty today (totaling more than 8 million individuals), compared with roughly 9 percent of whites (totaling more than 17 million individuals), 19 percent of Hispanics and 10 percent of Asians, while the clear majority of impoverished blacks, whites and Hispanics—between 54 percent and 65 percent—experience persistent poverty. And though a racial wage gap remains, the median earnings for all American workers is well below the median income forty years ago. See Leah Sakala, "Breaking Down Mass Incarceration in the 2010 Census: State-by-State Race/Ethnicity," Prison Policy Initiative, May 28, 2014, prisonpolicy.org/reports/rates.html; Cedric G. Johnson, "The Panthers Can't Save Us Now: Anti-policing Struggles and the Limits of Black Power," *Catalyst* 1(1) (2017): 57–85; Henry J. Kaiser Foundation, "Poverty Rate by Race/Ethnicity," Kaiser Family Foundation, 2016, kff.org.